# Clowning Around with Prostate Humor

Tony Deal

ISBN: 0615586872
ISBN-13: 9780615586878

# DEDICATION

To my wife Jennie and to the thousands of wives who "stand by their men" when things get tough

# CONTENTS

# ACKNOWLEDGMENTS

Not enough room to acknowledge all the people who encouraged me to create this book. I want to acknowledge my wife who offered suggestions and kept me from going too far out of bounds; Geoff and Dave at *485 Inc.* for the cover design; Gene for laughing with me; and Adam and Carrie for their support and ideas.

# Preface

**Question:**    Why prostate humor when cancer is so serious?

**Answer:**    Unlike the $87.52 prescription, humor is free, possibly just as effective, and doesn't have to be approved by one's insurance.

I believed in humor's power to heal but never experienced it until fate gave me the opportunity to see, up-close and personal, how laughter can change one's medical outcome.  With a diagnosis of prostate cancer, I began wandering through the medical maze with my underwear down to my knees, trying to keep some semblance of dignity and challenging myself to "perceive" as much humor as possible in not-so-humorous situations.  I was determined not to feel like a victim, to stay upbeat, and to use the power of humor to my advantage.

I also had a secondary reason for approaching prostate cancer in a humorous way.  Having worked with Hospice for over twenty-five years, I had observed how the diagnosis of cancer changed how we communicate with one another---especially if the cancer had to do with our sexual parts.  You seldom are treated the same once people know that you have the big "C."  People don't know what to say and too many times will put their feet in their mouths.  I ran into a female colleague who heard that I had prostate surgery.  With words of assurance, she told me to hang in there.  "Hang in there" might not be the best choice of words considering the *condition my condition* was in. So one good way to avoid those awkward comments is to "put it all out there" in a humorous way. I announced my diagnosis to family and friends in a tongue-in-cheek letter. I was pleased with how good I felt after laughing at my situation and the ease in which others could talk to me. I kept writing.

So six months and twenty-two chapters later, it's all on paper. I held back very little. "Damn if I would've told that" was a frequent response from other males. But it is as it is. Everything I tell is based on truth— from the joys of the biopsy, to my luxurious stay in the hospital, to my awkward attempts at sexual rehabilitation and to the daily challenges of "stress incontinence." Did I exaggerate some things? Well, yes! Sometimes the truth is dull and needs a little polishing. But most is told as it happened. Truth is not only stranger than fiction but also funnier. Look upon my story as a caricature of my experience. If you want a realistic, personal, yet funny experience of dealing with prostate cancer without having to bend over, look no further. I've done it for you.

As we grow older and have health issues, our challenge is to look for humor, nurture it, share it with others, and use this gift to its fullest. Remember that humor, like beauty, is in the eye of the beholder. It is there for the taking. So I hope you laugh with me. And when faced with a challenge, I hope you laugh at yourself. Just laugh at what is. You'll be glad you did!

*"If you don't learn to laugh at trouble, you won't have anything to laugh at when you are old."*      Will Rogers

# THE DIAGNOSIS

*Why my prostate and I are no longer buddies.*

For years, my prostate and I have been friends. Ever since I was thirteen, we had each other's back. I could always count on it during those special times. An old ally, now an enemy. That's what my urologist said. So after all these years, my prostate and I must part ways.

But I'm getting ahead of myself. Let's back up and begin at the beginning. To be perfectly honest, my saga began with a lie. I was in the examination room waiting to get my annual physical from my crusty, old male doc when in walked a young, attractive female nurse practitioner. "I'm covering for the doctor today." My first reaction, which did not come from my pre-frontal cortex, was "Wow, this is great!" But then I remembered that Doc ended each checkup by putting on those blue rubber gloves and giving them a little pop.

Would she or wouldn't she? Suddenly my heart rate and blood pressure changed. Once the rubber glove test came into my mind, she no longer had my full attention. Could I let this attractive woman give me the "ol' rubber glove test"? Decision time.

After the usual "stick out your tongue and cough" exam, she asked, "Do we need to do a digital prostate exam?"

Pausing only a millisecond, I offered up a bald-faced lie.

"I don't think so. I just had one recently."

Well, that's the best I could come up with on the spur of the moment…"just had one recently." Where would I have "just had one recently"? One would think we were talking about a cup of coffee. "No thanks, just had a cup." Glad she didn't ask where. On second thought, it would've been interesting to see where my second lie would have taken us.

So I skipped the digital exam, an exam that is "the" best predictor of prostate cancer. A year later, I assumed "the position," heard the popping of the gloves, and listened to my doc say, "Hmm, wish we had caught this earlier." Well, we could have---had she not been so attractive.

Doc's index finger discovered that my prostate was not in the same shape as the plastic prostate model on the desk. Being a family doctor, he referred me to a urologist. The urologist, not trusting the referral report, wanted to see for himself. So his index finger found what he called an asymmetrical prostate.

"Yep, there's a problem, but we won't know the extent until we do a biopsy."

*OK, that sounds simple enough,* I thought to myself.

He continued. "The good news is that with today's technology, we don't have to have an open incision to reach the prostate."

Great!  Sounds good so far.

I'm not big on anatomy but quickly concluded that without an incision, getting to my prostate would involve some portal, some existing opening, hopefully the largest and closest to the prostate.  I was correct on all counts.

On a chilly March morning, I showed up for what turned out to be my first of many "this may be a little uncomfortable," medical experiences.  From a medical perspective, nothing ever hurts like hell---it's just a little uncomfortable.

I was given a short "what-to-expect" briefing about the biopsy procedure and was immediately taken back to the refrigerator room where I discarded my warm clothing.  So there I was, wearing nothing but my socks and a paper napkin with sleeves.  They placed me on a cold table in an awkward and uncompromising position—a position that made a convenient workstation for the technicians.  I only saw the floor and an occasional foot passing by.  My sensory input was limited to touch (way too much of that) and sound.

Conventional wisdom portrays medical practitioners as often cold and insensitive toward their patients.  Well, trust me, that was not my experience.  They were too friendly for what they were doing and where they were doing it.  I'm sixty-seven.  Those of you who are my age understand that everyone in the medical field appears to be a teenager, especially the females.

After several minutes, a cheerleader came in, introduced herself, and said, "Mr. Deal, I'm first going to tell you what I am going to do, then I am going to describe what I am doing as I do it, and we will talk about how you are feeling as we proceed."

Whoa! Way too much information. Forget the small talk. Could we do this with a bag over my head?

She proceeded with "To begin with, I will be applying some…"

Considering the position I was in, I knew nothing good was going to follow the sentence that contained the words, "KY Jelly." I was right.

She continued, "You will feel some slight pressure and mild discomfort."

And the Mayor of Hiroshima said, "What was that noise?"

And they're off! Two stainless steel instruments racing side-by-side up the enclosed track toward my prostate. About halfway through the race, the young sonographer asked, "Are you OK? How are you feeling?" Not being sedated, I quickly realized that anything I said in response to a KY-Jelly-related procedure could be taken the wrong way, as in "Have you quit beating your wife?" How am I feeling? The word "good" wouldn't work. Give me a moment here. I was afraid that even my pause communicated something. I just grunted---hoping she would interpret it to my advantage.

5

I think steel horse # 2, named "Field of Vision," came in first place because I heard her say they had a good photo finish at the prostate. Suddenly everything stopped---except my heart.

"Mr. Deal, I am going to step out a moment but we have to leave these in until the doctor comes. Try not to move."

Try not to move! If ever there were wasted words, those words would top the list. From the depths of my being, I was trying not to move. What did she think I would do when she stepped out---the hokey pokey?

About this time I began to get a little paranoid. I am alone with just my thoughts. Fact: Extreme vulnerability enhances feelings of paranoia. Words started rambling around in my head, "step out," "leave these in," "when the doctor comes."

*What is left in? What is sticking out? Did she leave the door open? I feel a draft. Am I next to the waiting room? Whose footsteps are those? Do I hear people giggling?*

Then a big "Aha!" moment came tumbling in. Considering what the staff literally and figuratively face week after week, surely they add a little humor here and there to keep sane. I started thinking about what some of my "friends" would do if they were the "A-team" with emphasis on the A. Started thinking about *Mash*. So again, the thought, *What was in, what was out, who was in and who was out*, started to ring in my ears. Guess we will never know, but somehow I got the feeling that I was literally the butt of someone's joke.  Wonder what that single flower in the bud vase was used for?

Once the mini track-hoe was able to snag twelve bites of my prostate, the teenager said, "Mr. Deal, we are now going to slowly remove everything.  Try to relax."

*Try to relax* comes in as number two behind, *Try not to move*.

"Are you feeling OK?"  Total silence on my part.  Not falling for that question again.

The stainless steel horses were back in the stable, and I was sitting up.  No question that these people were sensitive, so sensitive that I felt like leaning against the gurney and smoking a cigarette.

# THE BIOPSY RESULTS

*"We have all your tests back and have good news and bad news. The good news is that your cholesterol seems to be down a bit. The bad news is...*

From a Buddhist perspective, there is no such thing as bad news, just news. So I got news. My brain's job was to try to comprehend the technical information being delivered by a white-coated, laptop-toting, uncomfortable physician whose knee and leg was going up and down so fast my first thought was of an alternative energy source.

"Mr. Deal, your PSA score, coupled with the biomarkers PCA3, do not support the existence of benign prostatic hyperplasia, but these data, plus your Gleason Score, indicate, by studying the immunohistochemical stains from the biopsy taken from the right lateral midregion of the prostate, the presence of prostatic adenocarcinoma. "

Well I'll be damned. That's exactly what my buddy down at the service station said you would say. The two of you really nailed it! Fred will be happy to know he was right. Guess he will collect the twelve bucks he won on the "Tony's diagnosis pool."

I think my prostate would be proud to know it is the subject of such enormous, educated, and powerful words. I guess that is better than saying "Mr. Deal, you've got one really screwed up prostate." So after mentally spraying down the cautiously optimistic euphemisms and technical data, out washed the fact that "Yep, you've got it, and you got it good. Could be worse though."

Now that we were through playing what's behind the biopsy door, it was time to say the magic word and win $100. Audience, the magic word is...options. That's right, ladies and gentleman, the word is OPTIONS. Doc started talking about all the options I had. So let's go straight to the options wheel and see what we have.

# THE OPTIONS WHEEL

*My wife voted for granite counter tops.*

**"Mr. Deal, one of our advanced options is not covered by your insurance, so you will have to pay an extra $6,000 to be assured you won't have erectile dysfunction following surgery. I realize that is a lot of money, so talk it over with your wife and let me know."**

**Well, I talked it over with my wife, and she would rather have granite counter tops.**

Note: My wife said to make sure that everyone knows this is a joke! But it isn't a joke for those without good medical insurance.

According to the doc, there are generally three categories of contestants making treatment choices. Two have clean and clear options, an unquestioned trajectory towards treatment. For the third category, well...that one is confusing to say the least. And guess where I landed. Let me explain.

Contestant One is a healthy, young male (65 and under) with a long life expectancy. So, for this contestant, aggressive treatment is a no-brainer. Select a door and go for it.

Contestant Two is old (70 plus) and usually unhealthy. Since prostate cancer is slow growing and probably will not interfere with one's life for ten plus years, these patients are usually sent home with the expectation that they will not outlive their prostate cancer. The blunt truth for this contestant goes something like this:

"Hey, you smoke, are over-weight, have diabetes and have not let go of the TV remote for 35 years, so go lie on the couch until the 'big one' hits."

Or

"Congratulations, you will not die from prostate cancer...because you won't be around long enough. See the actuarial tables on the back of the door as you leave."

Conveniently beside the actuarial table is an amortization table, so you can coordinate your medical payment schedule (drawn out over a 15-year period at 4.75 percent interest) with your life-expectancy. The perfect scenario is that you drop dead returning from the mailbox after you just made your last hospital payment. Remember, if you die before your cancer spreads, you win!

Of course, my contestant type would be the confusing one. I am a candidate for either no treatment or major treatment. I'm too old to be like contestant one and too healthy to be like contestant two.

"Mr. Deal, your problem is that you'll probably live too long. You are too healthy for your age. We are not sure what would be your best option. But you do have options."

Since starting this odyssey, I have had the suspicion that I was not the normal 67-year-old. Right after they made copies of my insurance cards, they handed me a pen (sponsored by Viagra), a clipboard, and four sheets asking about my medical history. The nurses continually asked me to bring in all my medications, to list on the back the number of times I get up to urinate during the night, my

13

previous operations, and my medical history. I check "none" or "never" on all of them and hand it back. "Mr. Deal, you forgot to list your medications." I could hear them in back, "Poor thing doesn't even know what he is taking." Next time I am going to put on the sheet, "I take Prozac for my mental health and Ex-lax for constipation. Sometime I forget and take too many pills and have to sit on the commode for long stretches...but I feel really good about it."

**Joke:** What do you get if you exercise daily, don't smoke, eat right, and make healthy lifestyle choices? Answer: You get three more years in a nursing home at a cost of $45,000 a year. Hey, that's not funny.

Now here is the kicker. After having talked to at least four doctors who specialize in either urology or oncology, not one, not a single one suggested what I should do. They were great at going over all the options, handing me slick glossy brochures with graphic pictures of those "hard to get to places," providing DVDs, and recommending websites that might enlighten me as to my options. At this point, I could lecture beginning medical interns at Johns Hopkins on the treatment options for prostate cancer.

> "As your dentist, I must inform you of all your options. I realize your tooth hurts, but you must to decide whether you want me to pull it, fill it, put a crown on it, give you a good cleaning, or refer you to the tooth fairy. I'm going to give

you a little time to decide. Tell the hygienist what option you pick."

"Yep, your car is broke alright. Won't go nowhere without fixing. Let me know if you want me to change the transmission, rebuild the engine, change the oil, or replace the windshield wipers. I can do whatever you tell me to do. You got lots of options."

# DECISION TIME

*"Would you rather make love to your wife or play with your grandchildren?"*

*"I hope I'll be feeding my grandchildren on our new granite counter tops."*

In keeping with the game show format, I will not reveal my "This is my final options choice," until I explain why I have rejected some of the other "treatment options."

Treatment Option I:   Active Surveillance (Watchful Waiting) or Playing Jack-in-the-Box.

Remember as a kid we would sit on the floor, put this tin box between our legs, crank a handle while listening to "Pop Goes the Weasel." With a sense of "watchful waiting," we would turn the handle slower and slower until out Jack popped (holy crap!), wobbling his weird clown head. Well, Active Surveillance is much like that. Apparently, you watch your prostate and stop cranking the handle just when you think it is about to pop out and invade the rest of your body. At that point you proceed to plan B—whatever that is. Doc says this treatment approach hopefully buys you more time in the saddle—whatever that is.

I am no expert on this stuff, but I see several flaws with this approach—flaws that beg questions like: Who watches? How often do they watch? What are they looking for? How do they know Jack is not just around the corner?

The experts have already told me that the PSA test is very unreliable; and I ain't playing the stainless steel horses again (as described in chapter I). That pretty much leaves one test to determine if "anything" is happening down there. That test is the old rubber glove, cold K-Y, index finger, digital exam. Checking my prostate every 3,000 miles for several years will involve large medical bills unless I could somehow conduct my own "watchful waiting exams" and bypass the medical community. Just how complicated could it be? I'm sure there is a YouTube video out there somewhere.

Let me digress. What are friends for? I have a lot of "so-called" friends and relatives who have said, "Sorry to hear about your illness. If there is anything, anything I can do, just let me know." Well, there just may be.

Did you know that it is impossible to lick your own elbow? I'm getting to a point here. If you want your elbow licked, you will have to call on a friend. Metaphorically speaking, I may need my elbow licked. A woman can easily do her own breast exam and can also easily get plenty of assistance just by the asking. We men are just one phone call away. "If there is anything we can do to help, just let us know...and we mean it!" But we men are not so fortunate. OK, maybe it is physiologically possible to self-examine one's own prostate. I'm at the theoretical stage here and have not thought through the logistics. Well, to be perfectly honest, I have tried to visualize possibilities, and it was not a pretty sight. So, where are my male friends who said they would do "anything" to help?

I got a pencil and started to list my many male friends and relatives whom I can count on to step up to the plate in my time of need. Coming up with potential volunteers was easy. Without much strain, I started writing down friends' names: Gene, Smithy, Sam, Bob, Donald, Gary, Larry, Rick, George. As I paused and looked at the list, I realized that I was looking at charter members of the "Hey Y'all, Watch This" Club. It would be advantageous to do some screening of my potential volunteers. My executive functioning forebrain decided to add a few filters. I would exclude anyone who:

1) Emailed back with, "Hell yeah, when do we start?"
2) Responded with, "How many slots do you still have open?"
3) Asked who was bringing the beer.
4) Offered to bring some buddies.
5) Played the banjo. (No empirical data to support this but a strong intuitive hunch.)
6) Fanned his face with his hand when excited.
7) Wanted to video it for a Facebook page.

As you can guess, my list of volunteers quickly diminished. After chewing the end off my pencil, all I had on the paper were nine scratched out names. Disappointing! But after a little reflection and applying the Golden Rule, I asked myself, "Would I do unto others what I was asking them to do unto me?" Then it hit me. I'm on my own with this "Active Surveillance" thing. Unless there are some esoteric, tantric yoga poses that I am not aware of, Option I was not in the cards.

That is...unless I suddenly get a ground swell of volunteers. I'll put a blog on the web and see what happens. May try E-Harmony. Send pics of your dominant hand.

## Episode 5

# MORE OPTIONS

*"Madam, would you like your garage door opened?"*

O ption I, Active Surveillance, is out. Not enough perverted friends. I'll describe some of the other common options and the reasons for their rejection.

Option II. EPBRT or External Proton Beam Radiation Therapy. I like the way they slapped the word "therapy" on the end of something that is designed to burn your prostate to smithereens. *Laser/computer guided radiation, pinpoint accuracy, little if any collateral damage*…wait a minute. Their little glossy brochure sounds a lot like what we heard during the "shock and awe" campaign in Iraq. According to the military spokesman, the laser-guided missiles had pinpoint accuracy. However, two weeks later we learned that a wedding party two miles away were counted as collateral damage. Interesting how they never fire those pinpoint accurate missiles when something of "vital interest" is nearby. Well guess what, according to Captain Johnson, there is something of "vital interest" near my prostate. No zapping in that area allowed. To be perfectly honest, I am not real comfortable with these new modern, self-flushing urinals that have a flashing red light pointed straight toward your…zipper. I may already be getting therapy from a urinal. Big Brother may be gathering information; he knows when I arrive, how close I stand to the wall, how long it takes me, and when I leave—thanks for the self-flush but no thanks. Point your EPBRT machine in some other direction. I'll pass on this one.

Option III.  Brachytherapy.  This "therapy" involves placing radioactive seeds in the prostate.  The brochure skips over a minor detail like how they get them in there and goes straight to possible side effects.  I am not real comfortable walking around with my private parts emitting radioactive waves.  Who knows all the implications...walk down the street and inadvertently open all the garage doors on the block.  And the airport TSA officials will really get excited when I step into their little cubicle and start firing back at them for a change.  I'll pass on this one also.

Option IV.  Cryotherapy   Truth is stranger than fiction.  You can't make this stuff up.  I quote directly from the brochure. *"Freezing gases drop the temperature of cryoprobes to minus 40 degrees Centigrade, thereby creating ice balls that freeze the entire prostate and some of the nearby tissue.  Warm saline solution is circulated through the urethra and bladder to protect them from freezing."*

Call me overly cautious, but I'm not going to participate in any treatment that has the phrase "ice balls" in the literature.  Related trivia quiz:  How did the saying "Cold enough to freeze the balls off a brass monkey" originate?  Answer:  Cannon balls were stacked on a brass plate called a monkey; when it would become very cold, the brass would contract, and the cannon balls would roll off.  Is it drafty in here or is it just me?  I think I'll go get my jacket.


Option V. Radio Waves   This is one of the newer treatments. Not sure how this works but apparently the poor prostate is tortured by the 24-7 sound of Lawrence Welk and his band of renown.  I don't know how effective this treatment is, but I know I would surrender.  Questions:  Does the patient get to pick the station? Commercials?  Could they use my Ipod?  If so, where would it be located?  Would I start humming the "Beer Barrel Polka" each time my wife and I became romantic?   So many questions, too few answers.  I'll pass on this one also.


Option VI.  Hormonal Therapy   This is the most complicated and controversial of all treatments because it represents a microcosm of the relationship between man and woman.   Apparently the male hormone, testosterone, is involved in prostate cancer.   Prostate cancer likes meat, animal products, stockcar races, pornography, and high levels of testosterone.  For god's sake, don't get a TV remote near the prostate.   As one would imagine, prostate cancer hates anything that is female.  My doctor told me that I need to turn my prostate into a peace-loving, sensitive vegetarian.  Estrogen, the female hormone, is the archenemy of prostate cancer.   Wouldn't you know it?  So the battle of the sexes goes on at the deepest hormonal levels in the body. Hormonal therapy involves lowering testosterone and raising the levels of estrogen—through the use of drugs and lifestyle changes. This can be done without some of the side effects found with options II-V. Hey, sounds great. Right? Wrong, way wrong. You know all those drug commercials on TV where they tell you what great wonders the drug will do and then spend most of the commercial telling you the possible side affects? Well, welcome to hormonal therapy.

Ask your doctor if hormonal therapy is right for you. Possible side effects may include a sudden or uncontrollable desire to:

- purchase more shoes, change your wardrobe.
- personally hand-write thank you notes to all who asked about you.
- really listen and care when your wife tells you about her cousin's neighbor's new baby.
- cry when you get stopped for speeding.
- really think about what gift would be appropriate for your wife's birthday.
- turn off football games and spend the afternoon playing a board game with your wife or go shopping.
- attend baby showers with the neighborhood women.
- join a Zumba Class.

Sexual side effects may include:

- A reduction in sexual desire  (The one in the Fall will suffice.)
- A need to feel loved before making love.
- The desire to feel attractive before intimacy.
- Headaches.
- Increase in size and tenderness of the breast.

OK,  need I say more?


Option VII.   Computer Controlled Robotic Surgery,   aka laparoscopy

The name of this new computerized wonder machine is called "da Vinci"---I suppose because of Leonardo da Vinci's knowledge of anatomy and his skill at designing machines.  If you don't have a life, Google "da Vinci" and watch people get their parts removed by this wonderful machine.   Since I'm close to running out of acceptable treatment options, I gave this much thought and consideration.  I was good at "pong" (the first computerized game ever invented) so I recognize the skill it takes to manipulate those little knobs.  I like my Wifi mouse and can see the possibilities of fine-tuned surgery.  However, before my forebrain had a chance to say yes, my primitive, intuitive, subconscious brain screamed "Hell no." The decision was made.  I would not do it.

Later I tried to understand my resistance to this wonderful technology and discovered that my brain was still fighting AT&T. OK, you are wondering what AT&T has to do with da Vinci. Well, it's all about outsourcing. I fell for AT&T's "bundling" scam and spent the better part of three days on the phone with Jagdish in India trying to explain that my new cell phone was not working at all. For three days he kept asking why I was unhappy with the quality of my calls, and for three days I tried to tell him I had no calls, no reception—nothing, nada, zilch, and without any reception, the quality of my calls would probably be less than desirable. We did not part friends. His last words were, "Sorry you have no good reception."

The da Vinci machine is computerized and the operator is not looking at your innards but is looking at a monitor. He could be in the next room, the next building, the next state or the next country. He could be in India. His name could be Jagdish. Jagdish could be moonlighting on the weekend doing prostate surgery and getting paid $7.00 an hour. No thanks. I want the one operating on me to be in the room, with his hands doing their thing on my thing.

Option VIII. Regular Surgery. Statistically speaking, I have used up my freedom of choice. (N-1 degrees of freedom) There ain't nothing left but the old fashioned, *Let's take a look in there and cut out what doesn't look like it belongs* Therapy.

So my choice was made. On May 4th at a major medical center, I was scheduled to say good-by to an old friend who turned enemy. One decision made---with little help from the doctors.

Having prostate cancer automatically put me into a research pool at a major state university. I understand using our tax dollars to research the causes and treatments of cancer. But at this university, their federally funded grant was studying the "quality of life" associated with prostate cancer—a quality that obviously goes south and it doesn't take our tax dollars to discover that.

I got a letter asking me to participate in their prostate cancer research. *Sure!* I signed my name and returned the form. About a week later, I got a call from some young co-ed (probably a work-study student) who said she was with the research project and wanted to ask me a few questions. We started. After the normal biographical stuff, we got straight into the meat of the matter (poor choice of words). For thirty minutes she asked about the past and present "quality" of my urinary and reproductive systems. As you can tell by my candor and bluntness in these blogs, I am a pretty open guy. I'm not ashamed to share some pretty personal stuff. Well, I wouldn't tell my wife some of the questions---much less my answers. Everything was on a scale of one to five. Some things just can't be expressed by numbers. "If 5 represents when you were 16 years old, on a scale of one to five, how would rate your current……….. thirty full minutes of unbelievable questions. Later, if they gave me lots of pain medication or I got really drunk, I might tell a few buddies some of the questions. No one will ever hear my answers except the little co-ed.

I was telling a friend of mine about how blunt the questions were from the young female interviewer. He speculated that maybe some of the questions had been developed at a sorority party and added just to make the monotonous work-study job more interesting. Now that puts everything in a different perspective. Can't wait until she calls again. The only thing worse would be my trying to explain the answers to Jagdish in India.

**Episode 6**

---

# THE PRE-OP EXAM

*"Brother, would you bend over just one more*

*time?"*

OK, the date has been set, tests run, and I thought we were ready to do the deed. Not quite. There is one more hurdle that I must jump, the Pre-op Evaluation---and jumping over hurdles with your pants around your ankles is not easy. The hospital scheduled me to meet with seven different "disciplines" so each one could "have its way" with me.

Hey, I've got a good idea, why don't you guys share with each other the information that you have, and I won't have to answer the same questions seven times, drop my pants six times (The business office did not have any rubber gloves in stock at the time) and show my insurance card each time I re-enter the building.

My first station was with the surgeon. But before seeing the real doc, a want-to-be physician who was doing his residency came in and started asking the same old questions I had answered twenty times. The fact that he had difficulty speaking the king's English did not seem to deter him. I nodded a lot. His eyes and attention kept jumping back and forth between the computer screen and my charts—flipping the pages hoping for information about why the hell this patient is in room 214. After about five minutes, he said, "Ah, I see you have prostate cancer and you are going to have surgery." I bit my tongue to keep from saying, "No shit, Sherlock. You are really good." Having spent his allotted time to qualify for an insurance payment, he left. Ten minutes later the surgeon came in, a great doc and human being. But true to my expectations, he wanted to check my prostate one more time. Do you think it has moved or decided to disguise itself as something else? "Yep, there it is." Always in the same place.

"You can stand up now, take these forms to the reception desk and go to station two."

Station two was obviously a holding pattern to keep you busy until station three was ready. This hospital must be competing with their cross-town rivals in things other than basketball because I was given a "quality of life" questionnaire similar to the one that the young co-ed asked me about. I took the clipboard with the pen attached and started on my seven pages. The room was crowded, so I had to sit beside a couple that had also just started on their seven pages. The only problem was that Mr. Highschool Dropout could not read, so his wife read each question to him. And obviously "Mr. Dropout" also had a hearing problem because his wife had to repeat each question.....all 53 of them.

"On a scale of one to five, how often have you…? Did you hear me?" I said, "On a scale of one to five, how often have you…?" for seven long, double-sided pages. I'm a little A.D.D. so I'm sure I put down his answers as many times as I put my own. Nobody reads them anyway.

Station three was a nice place; they let you go to the bathroom---in a plastic cup. Thank goodness. I was given a "kit" to collect the urine sample—a kit that did not have all the parts. Thanks, China! Instructions: "Tear open the plastic sterilized wipe and clean your....." There was no sterilized wipe in my kit. And the "sterilized wipe" was step two as was written on the back of the door. So, what to do? My pants are around my knees again, and I'll be damned if I am going back out into the reception area. So I made do. Did you know that the wall mounted electric hand dryers are multi-purpose? All's well that ends well.

A nurse thanked me for my urine sample and pointed to a room down the hall, told me to go in and wait---"wait" being the operative word. She forgot to say, "Wait till hell freezes over" because that's about how long I was in there. I had begun to doubt myself and wondered if I were in the wrong room---a room that no one was ever going to come into and from which no one would ever leave. I envisioned skeletons in the corners still holding their charts. Just as I was about to exit, two nurses came in---two nice looking nurses. Things were looking up.

Each time I had to answer personal questions to prove who I am. It's a good thing because I'm sure there were a lot of muggings and impersonations going on so they could take my place. "Hey, let's pretend to be Tony Deal so we can have our prostate removed. That'll be cool."

Never really understood why I was seeing the two nurses. They asked lots of questions that they had the answers for if they had only read my chart. Then they asked if I had any questions for them. Considering what they asked me, I thought it would be only appropriate if I asked them the same questions about their sexual and discharging systems. *On a scale of one to five, with one being never, how often do you...?* I didn't have the guts and didn't want to stay longer than necessary. However, they did remind me that I should shower, using their special soap, the day before and the day of my surgery and that I did not need to shave; that they would be shaving me here in the hospital. How nice, I hate shaving in the mornings.

Station four had potential. A very attractive female PA came in. As I was beginning to unloosen my belt, she asked me to sit on the examination table. She stuck a wooden popsicle stick in my face and asked me to open wide and say "ahh." With a stick in your mouth, it's difficult to say, " Honey, I'm not sure what you are looking for but I think you have the wrong end." She found the right end. Since the prostate is directly tied to one's sex life, many of the "How are you doing lately?" questions concern sexual matters.

"Mr. Deal, during the last 10 days, how often have you felt sexually aroused?" I paused, tried to recollect the last ten days. "Can I count this exam as one"? Where has our sense of humor gone?

Station five was wonderful. God bless a large black man named Peter from Kenya who had a big smile, a big heart, a sense of humor, and a laugh that would set anyone's soul free. His job was to draw blood. He asked me to sit down, roll up my sleeve. As he put on his blue rubber gloves, I asked if I should bend over. At first he looked confused, but then he caught the joke and started laughing— laughing so loud you could hear him at station two. Tears were rolling down his cheeks. He slid his stool back to the middle of the room to compose himself. Then he started telling a story about a woman who seriously asked if there was a different way they could check her husband's prostate other than having people put their finger up her husband's rear end. Did she seriously think there was a choice among several options to check the prostate and that physicians would choose the rubber-glove option?

"Let's see, I can use a specialized computer assisted scanner or a robotic laparoscopic technique or an x-ray assisted phototon, or I can stick my finger up the patient's rear-end. Now, which will it be? Hey, I think I will..........that'll be fun." We all wish there really were another choice.

Mr. Kenyan started laughing at his own story and could not stop. We both started laughing. People were sticking their heads in the door to see what was going on. He really lifted me up. I was a different person for the rest of the day.

He walked me to station six, shook my hand and was laughing as he left. Station six was no laughing matter. We are talking worse-case scenario. Please sign these forms indicating that you have been told all the possible things that can go wrong. Sign these forms releasing us of any responsibility. Sign these forms telling us who to call in case of … Sign these forms so we can release your records to the insurance companies. We need your power of attorney form, your living will, your health care bill of rights, the password to your MasterCard, the title to your motorcycle, and the warranty to your clothes dryer.

You get about five seconds to read a full page, size ten font, single-spaced document and sign it. Who knows what it really said and what I signed. Anyway, I was still on a high from station five.

Station seven was a piece of cake. This time all I had to take off was my shirt for the chest x-ray.

"Take a deep breath and hold it. You're done. See you May 4th."

I wonder how much this Pre-Op cost us taxpayers. Seems so inefficient. We all could have been in the same room, asked all the questions one time, dropped my pants only one time. They could take turns with me.

Yet I don't regret a dime that goes to pay the smiling Kenyan. With him, we got our tax-dollars' worth.

# PREPARING FOR SURGERY

*Out on a Limb of Mt. Zion's*

*Prayer Tree*

**Note:** I'm writing this chapter a few days after surgery. So, if in the middle of a sentence, I inadvertently type, "Yikes#$^&...," it is because I am having something called a "bladder spasm." They did not tell me what it was or how to prevent it ---just that I would know it when it occurred. Take two pills. They were right.

When the word got out that I had prostate cancer, the bugle was blown and the "soldiers of the cross" lined up—especially the troops from Mt. Zion's Women's Auxiliary. Here is all I know, and it ain't much. A nice lady asked if my name could be added to their pyramid prayer tree. My hesitation in responding revealed that I didn't have a clue what that meant and that I was afraid that somewhere down the chain I would end up selling Amway. She explained that within six weeks, I would have over 800 women praying for me. In short, they were going to worry God to pieces so SHE would not forget little old me. Like all good battle plans, theirs is waged on two fronts, one involves the prayer tree and the other involves prayer shawls. I admit up front that I don't fully understand the prayer thing, yet the women of Mt. Zion sure seemed to have it figured out.

I vaguely remember from my Religion 101 Class about prayers of intercession. In short, these prayers work like a public relations lobbyist who helps God make up her mind, change her mind, and/or ensure that God does not get distracted by big ticket, international disasters like the earthquake in Japan and forget the local scene. "OK, ENOUGH ALREADY. I WILL DEAL WITH IT. JUST STOP CALLING IN." It must be like turning over your prayer concerns to a debt collection agency or a Washington lobbyist.

I remembered the Jewish joke in which a little old lady stood up in the middle of a funeral and shouted, "Give him some chicken soup." The rabbi said, "Madam, I'm afraid that can't help." She yelled back, "Can't hurt!" So my brain yelled, "It can't hurt." Not sure what tree or limb I'm on, but I'm on there somewhere.

Just in case someone breaks the chain, another regiment is knitting a prayer shawl. This shawl is about five inches wide and six feet long. Like a mantra, each stitch is put in with a word of prayer. With literally thousands of stitches, the prayer could not be very long or I will be 103 years old before I get to put the shawl on or around something. They never did go into detail about how I was to use the shawl. Just know it is made with love. Maybe my banjo picking buddies could start tying knots in their instrument straps, and with each knot, make a wish for something good to happen to me. The women of Mt. Zion would faint seeing that list.

Regardless of how traditional prayer or being held in the light works, I am grateful for it. On some level, I know it may help. Can't hurt.

While my church friends were waging a holy public-relations war, the medical community was also ensuring that my body, if not my soul, would be "cleansed."

Cleanse, Cleanse, Cleanse. Those words are shouted each morning on a local radio station—selling some herbal remedy referring to a colon cleanse. Obviously, my doctors listen to the WKGX morning show because their cleansing regimen started two days before surgery. Think you know how to take a bath? Wrong. You need to get the brochure on how to wash your body the day before and the day of surgery. Think you have good soap? Wrong. Throw out that sissy, hypo-allergenic, no tears Mr. Bubbles and get a real man's soap. Think your intestines are cleansed with a daily tablespoon of Metamucil? Wrong. Wait until you drink their chemical concoction that makes Metamucil seem like processed cheese.

Like the two campaigns waged by Mt. Zion, the doctors two campaigns involved internal and external cleanse, cleanse, cleanse on the day before and the day of surgery.

On the day before surgery, I was instructed to cleanse my insides by drinking the bottle of mystery liquid. Very little instructions except to drink the entire bottle the day before surgery. I was also instructed to wash my body the day before surgery. Check and double check. Did both.

I really hesitate to criticize my hospital which is the best of the best. However, there are a few suggestions that they might want to consider during their next Total Quality Circle.

**Suggestion #1:** Have only one set of instructions within the same packet. This suggestion comes from the fact that men do not like to read instructions in general, much less try to determine which of the two directions they must follow. My external cleansing kit was literally a Ziplock bag with two hermetically sealed cleansing kits inside. Each kit had instructions on the back. Unbeknownst to me, there was another set of typed instructions under one of the packets, which began with, "ignore the instruction on the packets." I remembered they said to wash the day before and the day of my surgery. So the day before, I opened the Ziplock bag, took out the kit #1, read the instructions, and proceeded with the cleansing. OK, I admit I could be accused of "contributory negligence" because a big part of me was screaming "that doesn't seem right." Anyway, how was I going to use the fingernail cleaner that was included? But impatient and eager to get on with it, I proceeded to cleanse myself—given what I had before me and the instructions I was reading.

**Suggestion #2:** With written instructions, always bold and underline the words, **<u>Do not use on genitals</u>**. I'm not an English major but I'm sure the word "gentle" and the word "genital" both came from the same Latin root "genii" i.e., "to treat with tenderness."

On the day of surgery, I opened my Ziplock bag, took out kit #2 and discovered the "other" instructions. Surprise, surprise. The part of the new instructions that jumped off the page at me was, 1) Do not use the bristle side of the scrubber, 2) Do not use on genitals, 3) Discard fingernail cleaner. That information would have come in handy yesterday!

Let's go back to the mystery internal cleanser. Nowhere did it say when and how the liquid would take effect. Just take it the day before. At 4:00 PM, I drank the entire bottle and prepared myself for the internal cleansing that soon would follow. Five o'clock, six, seven o'clock rock, bedtime still nothing. Next morning, nothing. I was beginning to wonder if I took the right stuff. Later during the day, I turned my attention to kit #2 and decided to do the external cleanse. The newly found instructions were kinder, gentler than the ones on the kits. "Using the soft side of the sponge, cover your body from neck down (do not use on genitals) with the suds made by the soap in the sponge and let stand on your skin for three to five minutes." Reasonable enough. I looked like a member of the Blue Man Group but was orange. Just when I got completely covered (one thousand one, one thousand two) I heard a faint rumbling noise. Could not make out where it was coming from. I knew there was a train track in the nearby town of Carrboro. Focused my full attention on the rumbling---reminded me of the sound effects from Ghost Busters II. Then it hit me. The rumbling was coming from deep inside me. The mysterious internal cleanser has just spoken. Decision time. I've already waited for 14 hours; surely I can wait for four more minutes. Wrong! For goodness sake, don't slip getting out of the tub. I was staying at my sister in-law's new house and didn't want to pay to re-wallpaper her bathroom. In life, I occasionally make the right choice. I made one that day.

**Suggestion #3**: Print the following warning label on the internal cleanse bottle: Do not take if you plan to attend a wedding, funeral, any significant social event, or if you must turn your undivided attention to some action other than that proposed by this liquid.

OK. I'm clean inside and out. Let the surgery begin!

# CHECKING IN FOR

# SURGERY

*"Mr. Deal, Your Table Is Ready."*

I'm amazed that, after 67 years of being humbled by life, there is still an egocentric child inside me who expects the rest of the world to see "my crisis" as really important. Not sure what I was expecting when I arrived at the university medical center on the big day--- maybe a human to meet me personally, someone to walk me through what was going to happen, or someone to offer me a glass of warm milk and hold my hand as I crossed the street. Hope springs eternal. The fact that I was e-mailed a personalized bar-code the day before should have tempered my high expectations.

When we got to the pre-op staging area, my inner child wet his pants. We entered a place that looked and felt like a marriage between an airport terminal and an Olive Garden Restaurant. People were waiting everywhere. To keep track of us, we were given a restaurant style circular spaceship that lights up and vibrates when it is your turn—your turn either to be served or to be served up.

The spaceships were going off like lightning bugs in a summer sky. When mine finally buzzed, I was taken through the "No Admittance" double doors, walked passed stalls of terminal gall-stones, breasts, kidneys, knees, and who knows what other body parts were waiting for removal. My guide pointed to a stall, handed me a plastic personal effects bag and the traditional "expose your ass gown." I was told to strip, put on the gown and a pair of too small non-slip socks, and get in bed.

A real sense of helplessness came over me as I sat alone in that cold cubicle, behind a curtain, and only hearing the hurried commotion of people and machines. I suddenly realized, "This is serious business." Yet I remembered my challenge to find something humorous in every situation, and this was my first real test. These people were all business. No funny stuff here. Was I at the end of my little humor-writing gig?

Time alone offered me the opportunity to reflect on those who provided my previous humorous and uplifting experiences. My serious mood allowed me to get down on us "white folks" because it seemed that all my pleasant, uplifting, humorous, and human-to-human experiences had come from citizens of color. It didn't make any difference whether they were doctors, house-cleaners, nurses, transportation specialists, anesthesiologists, or secretaries---those of color seemed to have a spark, the darker the color the greater the spark. Is that true? Just as I was about to conclude my hypothesis was correct, the three "Andrews Sisters" arrived and blew my theory all to hell.

Outside my curtain a woman's voice called, "Mr. Deal, are you ready? Hey, let's make a deal, Mr. Deal."

Another voice said, "What do you think we will find behind curtain #2? Well, audience, let's find out."

And wham, the curtain slid open and in raced three nurses, who for the next fifteen minutes "had their way with me." These "white ladies" were balls of fire, upbeat, cracking jokes all while they were connecting me to yards of plastic tubing by using existing openings or making their own. One went straight to my left arm, the second to my right arm, and the third started asking me questions. I agreed to answer only if I could ask her questions in return.

"Honey, you can ask me anything you want."

And she meant it, so I didn't dare. Within no time, I was shaved (still had my beard), showered, shampooed, and prepared for action. As fast as they came in, they moved on, laughing, and vowing that they did not "have their way" with me. Fantasy #278 dashed! All they left behind was a relieved old man wearing a red hair net and extruding lots of plastic tubing. Wow! What a great 15 minutes. And to think I was "stuck and stabbed several times" and never even knew it. Is it physiologically impossible to laugh and feel pain at the same time?

My next visitor was the surgeon. After the usual "How are you feeling questions?" and general assurances, he asked, "Do you have any questions or concerns?"

"Well, yes, there is one. I know this may sound a little weird, but I would like to have my prostate to take home with me. I want to see the little bastard."

After my wife rolled her eyes and gave me that "I don't believe you asked that" look, and after the surgeon's "They don't pay me enough for this job" pause, he said, "I'm afraid that won't be possible. There's not enough time to sign the numerous consent forms the lawyers would dream up that would allow that prostate to leave this hospital."

When he realized I was serious, he said, "I'll take my camera into the operating room and take a picture for you." And he did. Watch out YouTube.

Next, I was visited by Dr. O, a foreign-born anesthesiologist whose name is so long that everyone just calls him Dr. O. I liked his "affect." After the usual reassurances, he asked about my hobbies. As we talked about my interest in bicycling, he rested his hand on my shoulder. What a simple but powerful gift. According to a nurse, Dr. O always wears crazy colored hats each day. His *chapeau du jour* was bright paisley with all the colors of the rainbow.

So into one of the portals (made by one of the "Andrews Sisters) went the jungle juice and out went the lights. My red hair net was replaced by a blue one and away I went. Only blue hair nets get cut on.

I know the jungle juice was a strong drug, but the real juice came from the smiles and jokes of the Andrews Sisters, the "going beyond the call" photographer surgeon and the reassuring touch by Dr. O. As they rolled me into surgery, the smile on my face came from humans—not the pharmacy.

# AFTER SURGERY

*"Nurse, what is that tube connected to?"*

My first memory after surgery was a nurse leaning over the bed.

"Mr. Deal, welcome back. You're in the recovery room. How are we feeling?"

OK, give me a minute here. Got to get oriented. How are "we" feeling?

No offense, but I don't know how I'm feeling much less how you are feeling. Four letter expletives keep coming to mind but they are not "feeling" words. Need some "feeling" words that are more than four letters.

To quantify the level of pain, nurses use a pain scale from one to ten, with one being equal to your leaning back on the headboard, lighting a cigarette and saying "Wow, that was great" and ten equaling "Shoot me, please." I realize they need quantifiable numbers for their records, but I don't know where "feeling like crap" falls on the number scale. Put me down as a six.

As I began my body scan, everything looked and felt good from the waist up. No problem there. Below the waist, well, that's another story.   No positive signals coming from my pelvic area. The white sheet covering my body presented some semblance of normalcy.   Besides being "uncomfortable" (we never have pain, we are only uncomfortable), everything seemed OK.   However, things went downhill with the words, "Mr. Deal, let's take a look at your incision."

Doc threw back the sheet and I gazed upon the war zone with disbelief.  Wow.  I was as hairless as a newborn baby, had weird looking sutures starting at my belly button and running as far south as one could go without trespassing into the Holy Land, had mounds of stomach fat clustered into what looked like moguls on a ski slope. You know those stories about doctors mistakenly leaving things in the patient during surgery; well, if anyone on my surgery team can't find his Ipad, I have a suggestion of where to look. Wait a minute, *What's that tube doing where it has no business being?   Who authorized that?    Surely, I did not sign for that to happen.*   Out of literally thousands of words available for my brain to choose from, only "damn" seemed to fit the moment.

OK, here is where the sensitive among you might want to skip ahead a few pages because the issue of the Foley Catheter has to be addressed.  It is the elephant in the room.   As I lay back on my pillow and took several deep breaths, I recalled someone mentioning something about a Foley Catheter that would be in place seven to ten days after surgery.  And again, I will accept some of the blame for my complete denial of what those words really represented.   My

Buddhist teachings reminded me that words are only fingers pointing to the moon. Words are not the real thing. A Foley Catheter on paper is just that, an innocent Foley Catheter. What I got was something much different.

Reminded me of the time when I was building our house and was trying to convince an old, seasoned carpenter that we were not nailing siding the way I had read in a book. He listened but kept nailing the boards the way he had nailed them since his dad showed him. Pausing to spit out some tobacco, he said, "Son, a book will lay there and let you write anything in it." He kept hammering.

Well, those pre-surgery, medical assurance papers will lay there and let hospital administrators write all sorts of Pollyanna words and technical terms to describe what is going to happen. Their words seldom tell what really is going to happen, that is, from the patient's perspective.

To help me prepare for the real catheter experience, someone should have given me the following document to sign:

## Permission to Install a Foley Catheter

*This document seeks your permission to receive a Foley Catheter. After surgery, we are going to shove a hose up your penis all the way to your bladder. We will expand the bladder end of the hose so you can't pull it out, because we know you will try. The other end of the hose will be connected to a clear plastic bag so everyone can see how much urine you are passing. We will strap the bag to your leg so when you walk around, the sloshing sound will remind you to be careful to not get the hose caught on a piece of furniture. That would be uncomfortable.*

*Emptying the bag is no problem. Observe a male dog. Just raise your leg over the commode, open the valve and balance yourself on one leg while voiding. Be careful not to slip. You may want to change socks after each occurrence.*

*To keep from getting infections, you must change and wash the bags daily. Instructions come with each bag because each one is designed differently. Changing bags will require the assistance of a caregiver---someone with whom you will feel no shame and someone you trust. We also will give you a small travel collection bag in case you are stupid enough to go out in public. Just don't go far because the small bag is good for about 20 minutes. Getting the gallon sized bag down your pants leg without disconnecting anything will be a challenge, but we leave it to our patients to figure that one out.*

*Sleeping with the Foley is no problem. However, never, ever roll to the left if your catheter is attached to your right leg or bedside. Doing so will result in your being uncomfortable (8.5 on the scale). If by chance the tube becomes irritated or uncomfortable at the tip of your penis, you may want to use some localized painkiller on that spot.*

*On second thought, you absolutely will want to use some localized painkiller.*

*The catheter will be in place for approximately ten days unless we have to shift our appointment schedule which may result in Mr. Foley visiting with you for two or three weeks. Count on the latter. Please sign and witness below.*

My brother says that what happens in life should be viewed as a lesson to be learned. So here is what I have learned from Mr. Foley:

1) Pride is overrated. Shame is an old friend who visits often.

2) Trust is <u>not</u> over-rated. Whoever has the other end of the catheter is a cherished friend.

3) Agreements come naturally. It is so easy to say "Yes, Dear" to your wife when she is holding the other end of your catheter.

4) When walking to the bathroom, stay very close to the person carrying the other end of your catheter. Your full attention must be given to the distance between you and your catheter-wielding caregiver.

5) The catheter will cost you money—money other than health care dollars. For some odd coincidence, each time my wife is carrying the other end of my catheter, she thinks of something she needs, e.g., new dress, jewelry, etc., and asks

what I think. My instinctive answer: "Yes, Dear, that would be nice." She refers to my catheter as the "short leash."

6) I have a better understanding why a bridle and bit work so well in a horse's mouth. I will gee or haw whenever instructed to by my caregiver.

7) Words do count. They say "small plastic tubing" and I say "hose." If it looks like a duck, walks like a duck; if it feels like a hose…

As if the catheter experience is not humiliating enough, got a big ol' slap in my white man's face by the hospital. I really hesitate stumbling through this topic because there are so many "politically incorrect" landmines to blow up in my face. But if I am going to be honest about my entire saga, then I must address the fact that this whole ordeal has challenged my "white manhood" in many ways and in one way that was completely unnecessary.

*Newsweek Magazine* recently featured an article on how the white man is being challenged on every front, e.g. sports, politics, CEO positions, number of college graduates, income levels, etc. I admit that the white male has had it made for the last while, say a couple of thousand years or so. But don't we deserve to retain just a little sense of pride.

Here's the point. As if the above description of my catheter experience was not enough to challenge any white-man's dignity, the hospital decided to rub in a little salt along the way. Some female nurse (with a twisted sense of humor) had the wonderful idea of making a DVD that would demonstrate to the patient and his caregiver (usually the wife) how to care for, clean, and manage the catheter. Sounds innocent enough. So a nurse came in my room with a portable DVD player and a disc. My wife and I were instructed to watch the program as a couple. The nurse pushed all the right buttons and left. The program started.

"Welcome to the University Medical Center, We are happy to present... yada, yada, yada."

Then the program came on and sure enough, a real live person, with real live parts was featured using the close-up zoom. Took me a second to adjust to what I was seeing. I noticed that what was on that screen had my wife's full attention.

OK, let me stop here and ask a few questions. What is the ratio of men of color to white men in NC? If one were to randomly pick an actor for the video, there would be a high probability that the actor would be white. For every two citizens of color there are seven white men---seven that would be available to be on that video. Enough said. Some of you may get my point. I would have preferred that the item of interest would have looked like my item of interest. The video reinforced the widely held belief that white men don't come in first place in the "endowment" contest.

My wife asked if we could re-wind it. I started talking about Photoshop and the technical ability to enhance digital images. The nurse said the video was a gift, and it was ours to take home to look at as many times as necessary to fully understand the catheter. Big chance of that happening. Thanks a lot. If there is anything I can do to boost your ego, just let me know.

# Episode 10

# THE HEALING PROCESS

*Why we should be grateful for hippies.*

(Lyrics)

*Where have all the hippies gone, long time passing?,*

*Where have all the hippies gone, long time ago?,*

*Where have all the hippies gone, practicing medicine one by one?,*

*When will we ever learn, when will we ever learn?."* (Apologies to Joan Baez)

The peace, love and drug culture of the 70's has aged its way up the socio-economic ladder and now those dirty, bellbottomed, freaked-out flower children are attorneys, teachers, engineers, writers, and medical professionals. If you are a patient in pain, be grateful that those hippies traded one set of drugs for another. "Hey man, feeling some pain? Try a little of this." Yes, hospitals have changed.

During college I had a hospital experience resulting from a motorcycle accident—nothing serious just lots of road rash, contusion, cuts, etc. The hospital rationed pain medication as if J. Edgar Hoover himself would inventory their stash each day. You had to be screaming to get anything other than an aspirin. And it took a court order to get out of the place. They kept me as an in-patient until all the scares were gone. Whole semester shot to hell.

But thanks to today's professional hippies, those days have gone the way of the rainbow-striped VW camper.

> "Mr. Deal, we do not give any awards for suffering. Pain is not our thing. We have 'scored some good stuff' to make sure that your experience with us is pain-free. Anytime you feel that Mr. Pain is about to pay a visit, just push your call button."

Believe it or not, they now have self-dosing pain pumps that let you, the patient, decide when to take a hit. I was not allowed that luxury---probably because I was too truthful on one of those long questionnaires. Question: Have you ever used or tried....... Answer: Well, yes ......... That answer cost me about 30 CCs of something good.

I'm no medical expert, but somehow allowing the person to self-regulate does not seem to pass the smell test. Look around at the fat people in McDonald's and see how much self-regulation is going on. Remember those addiction experiments with monkeys? Three days after drug "self-regulation therapy," the monkeys were leaning against the wall, with big smiles on their faces, legs crossed, scratching their privates with one hand, and pushing the pain-pump with the other. The male monkeys would trade "time on the pump" for a little private time with some of the females. Nah, that protocol will never work. Won't work for monkeys or their descendants.

Yet I did have potential for pain. When your stomach muscles are surgically sliced, it only hurts when you try to sit up or sit down, bend over, walk, turn to the right or the left, laugh, cough, or sneeze. For all other movements you are "free to move about the cabin." As my yoga instructor says, "Your core is where it all happens."

The justification for all the pain medication is that you need to be active as quickly as possible after surgery to prevent something from happening. They never did tell me what it was that would happen. Don't get me wrong. I'm all for this new pain management plan.

I had no more than gotten my bed warm after surgery when a nurse asked, "Mr. Deal do you feel like walking a little?" Mental timeout: I just had surgery; I'm disoriented; feeling a little queasy; haven't eaten in 36 hours; have been internally cleansed, cleansed, cleansed; and am still at a loss as to what is hooked up to you-know-what.

I'm not sure how I answered her. I just remember my wife chastising me with, "She's just doing her job." So, apparently I gestured something that indicated my annoyance with the thought of strolling down the halls so soon after having my gut cut open.

The offended nurse must have notified the head nurse because five minutes later Ms. Clockwork Orange comes in with a medication plan to change my outlook.

"I understand you are uncomfortable. Let's see if this will help."

I challenged her ability to change my mind about walking. I responded, "Yeah, let's see."

And see we did. Fifteen minutes later I was happily cruising down the hall, hair uncombed, wearing nothing but my opened-back, faded blue gown, orange non-slip socks, waving to other patients, giving high-fives to passing visitors, and proudly showing off my half-full urine bag hung on the side of my walker. And my walker was cool—four wheels, armrests that allowed me to stand erect when my body was inclined to do otherwise, and had places to hang things. If I had owned that walker in college, I could've stayed longer at parties. A nurse's aide, walking several steps behind, gave on-lookers the slight impression of a parade. I think her job was to make sure that my hospital gown stayed open in the back at all times. We made several laps before I collapsed in bed.

# Episode 11

====================================================

# THE TREATMENT GOAL

*"Why is my suitcase setting on the sidewalk? I just got here."*

E ven though there were several treatment goals, obviously one of the main goals was to get me out of the hospital ASAP. I was back on the street in less than 24 hours. I think my medical protocol was called, "Get this Medicare patient off the hospital's dime as quickly as possible." Here is a scary thought. If the so-called wasteful Medicare Program results in only a one-night stay after major surgery, what will happen if the insurance companies are allowed to have their proposed voucher system? "Present this voucher for a 26 minute hospital stay after surgery--- and good luck to our most valued customer."

The "pain-free" and the "get up and walk" approaches helped justify my being medically discharged so soon after surgery. "Hey, you are pain-free and are up and walking. Don't see any reason you should stay any longer."

And if these two approaches were not enough to get me out, the hospital had a third key strategy that would seal the deal—a strategy to make me beg to go home. I call this tactic the "You really need it but you can't get it here" scheme. Here is how this played out for me.

The medical staff continuously stressed the importance of rest and good nutrition for healing. Then they made sure that you wouldn't get either while under their care.

During my first and only night's stay, someone would come in every two hours and ask if I were resting. "Mr. Deal, are you able to sleep?" Attached to both arms were several malfunctioning machines to monitor my vital signs—machines that would suddenly start beeping about every hour. I've seen too many emergency room TV programs to know that when a vital-sign machine starts beeping and radically changes sound, the drama begins. Several times during the night I expected the "blue team" to come running in and start shocking my chest. "Am I dying, or is the machine malfunctioning? Better call the nurse."

"Oh, it's just this machine. Try to go back to sleep."

If that were not enough, my lower legs were surrounded by some type of leg balloons that would blow-up, release, blow-up, release, all night long. Each time they reached their limit of air, the plastic would make a popping noise. The few times I dozed off, I would wake up thinking someone was trying to pull me out of the bed by my ankles. Sleep and rest were nowhere to be found. And I thought working the third shift in Cannon Mills was a long night.

I was glad to see the sun come up so I could have that good nutrition they talked so much about. I was ready for fresh fruit and yogurt, with granola sprinkled on top, followed by steel cut oatmeal with honey and organic almond milk, a small piece of wholegrain wheat toast and hot green tea. A good breakfast will start my day off right.

When breakfast finally arrived at 9:36 AM, I was beyond hungry. The brown plastic tray was covered with a heavy top, presumably to keep the delicious food warm. Wrong. The top was to hide the food. When I uncovered the tray, my heart sank as I viewed a rounded ice-cream scoop of powered eggs, one hard-as-a-rock waffle slice with make-believe syrup, one small slice of a cooked apple, a piece of white bread (which I haven't eaten in ten years) and something called juice-punch made with water, high fructose corn syrup, yellow dye # 2, red #5, blue #40, a variety of fruit juices from several Central American countries, and a long list of unpronounceable words. They gave me about ten minutes to be alone with my meal; then the nurse came back in.

"Mr. Deal, you look tired and you don't seem to be hungry this morning. Do you feel like going home today? We thought you might. Let's get those discharge papers started."

It worked. Their strategy #3 worked. Was I ever ready to go home! A nurse started unhooking me from all the machines and when finished, she offered up one more obstacle between me and home.

"Mr. Deal, before you leave, we would like to see you have a bowel movement."

Hey, at this point I'm up for anything, especially if Ms. Orange is involved. My asking who would like to watch did not go over very well. Obviously, I had misunderstood. She quickly rephrased her request.

Sedation or not, it didn't take me long to realize that I was in deep trouble. Let's review. Twenty-four hours before surgery, I was restricted from eating anything. Then I was given the "Ex-lax liquid from hell" that cleansed every particle from my colon. The day of surgery equaled no food. The powdered eggs did not result in anything significant going into my digestive tract. The "pretend-to-be juice" ended up in another lower-body compartment. And they wanted to see a bowel movement before I leave.

My son talks about the universe being created out of nothing, as in no-thing or emptiness. Well, that is exactly what must happen again if they want to see a bowel movement before I leave. Short of another cosmic miracle, a "movement" wasn't going to happen. I begged to be exempt from this one. They let me slide.

I had one last hurdle to jump before being set out on the sidewalk. As part of the "patient responsibility" guidelines, I had to educate myself on the correct procedures for being my own homebound nurse. The Sundance Film Festival entry #17, *Making Friends with Your Catheter*, had already been shown to my wife and me. I could check that one off.

I had to learn how to handle my incision, medications, Depends (a noun, not a verb) and personal hygiene. Obviously, the educational materials are written for the lowest common denominator among us humans. Again I may be crossing into the politically incorrect zone, but the Darwin Awards seem to be appropriate here. For example, if I die because I'm not aware that "peanut butter contains peanuts," then my death improved the human gene pool; therefore making me a candidate for the Darwin Awards.

**Instructions:** "Tear open package and use wipes as instructed." If I injure myself wiping my hard-to-get-to places with the aluminum package, I deserve the rash.

**Instructions:** "Do not take if you are allergic to contents." If I take it knowing I'm allergic to it, I deserve to swell up like a toad or to get my Darwin Award in heaven.

**Instructions:** "Do not use the thermometer orally if previously used rectally." I really needed that reminder.

**Instructions:** "Do not ride horses, bicycles or operate heavy machinery if the Foley catheter is still inserted."

Now that sentence is a waste of ink. If after major surgery and the catheter is still inserted into you-know-what, and some idiot thinks he wants to "ride a horse, bicycle or operate heavy machinery" then he deserves the consequences of said behavior. Thank you for improving the gene pool. Fast forward three weeks after surgery and I'm still sitting on a foam donut hole. The thought of riding a horse makes me nauseous.

Oh yes, I am to "take my pills by mouth three times daily, stopping when they are gone." Oh really? I thought I would take a few after they were gone to see what would happen. Will keep you posted.

So there I was, less than 24 hours after surgery, sitting on the sidewalk holding my catheter bag with one hand and clutching my prescription of oxycodone with the other.

"Hurry up and bring the car around before I get picked up as a vagrant."

**Episode 12**

=========================================

# THE TRIP HOME

*"What the hell was I thinking?"*

I've done my share of "Hey y'all, watch this" things---but agreeing to leave the hospital so soon after surgery ranks right up there at the top. In the outside world, the difference between my choosing something smart and something really stupid is about five beers. In the hospital, the difference is about two oxycodone tablets.

Obviously, I had swallowed my two pills because I was headed west on I-40, windows down, hair blowing in the wind. All was well with the world...well for the first several hours. I never was good at those math problems about a train leaving Chicago going 60 MPH and one coming from San Francisco at 50 MPH....etc. So obviously I failed this test question:

> If the half-life of one oxycodone tablet is 45 minutes, traveling at 55 miles per hour for 170 miles, when will Tony start painfully squirming if he takes two tablets all at one time, forty-five minutes before he leaves the hospital?

Give up? Well, I'll tell you the answer. Tony started squirming about 30 minutes before he got home. Fifteen minutes before he got home, he was entering the childbirth stage of transition—a stage that required Lamaze panting, blowing and cursing. Hats off to the real birthers.

You don't have to be a math whiz to know that I had royally screwed up. Two and a half hours into the trip home I could not find a comfortable position in that car seat. I had never noticed the roads being so bumpy and full of potholes. My wife suddenly became the world's worst driver.

"Damn it. Can't you see those holes? Slow down. No, speed up. Slow down! Can't you pass that slow bastard?"

"Cursing doesn't help."

"The hell it doesn't."

It's interesting that when we go beyond our pain threshold, our brain selects that one special word that must be mumbled as in some primal mantra. I had found mine. And I was not chanting what a devout wife was pleased to hear.

My wife, obviously not having an all-inclusive picture of my situation, had the gall to suggest that we pass our house, drive into town and go by the drugstore to get my prescriptions filled. And I'm sure she would have stopped to buy a few groceries. After a very short, one-sided little chat, she clearly understood the extent of my pain. Silence prevailed the last five miles as she drove straight home. I may have hurt her feelings. No, I'm sure I hurt her feelings.

Home is where the heart is, and home is where my own pain management skills would come into play. With a "little help from my friends," and a little help from my medicine and liquor cabinets, I put an end to my suffering. But not before I almost became unglued. I was in the bathroom balancing on one leg---trying to figure out how to get my pants off with the catheter tied to my leg and threaded through the pant leg, hurting all over, shaking with the chills, and questioning, "What the hell was I thinking?" when I agreed to leave the hospital after one day. This was by far the low point of my little saga.

Chalk it up: "Hey y'all, watch this" # 236.

# Episode 13

# HOMEBOUND REHAB

*"You ain't worth much…"*

"**M**r. Deal, for the next four to six weeks we don't want you to push, pull or lift anything more than ten pounds; don't drive if you still have a catheter. Beyond that, do what you normally do as long as it doesn't cause pain."

"Do what you normally do." The problem with that statement is that I don't normally sit on a sponge donut for sixteen hours, just getting up to empty "the bag." I normally don't go to bed at 9:00 PM because I'm bored to death. It's *Groundhog Day* all over again—what day is this anyway? Confession time: The last four weeks have been a difficult adjustment---especially for someone whose motor idles a little faster than most.

My lifestyle has been one of "doing" rather than "being." I never sit still for very long. Several years ago I checked my elementary school permanent folder to see the comments teachers made about me—made during a time when teachers were honest and blunt in an effort to warn next year's unlucky teacher. I found comments like "Will not sit still," "Too fidgety," "Need to keep him busy," etc. I guess that is why I spent much of my elementary years dusting erasers, taking out the trash, sharpening pencils, going to get the morning orange juice. I thought I had a personal tutor but it turned out to be the school janitor. Glad chalk dust was not carcinogenic, or I would have been a member of a class-action lawsuit by the time I was in the eighth grade. On second thought, maybe it was carcinogenic and that is why I'm sitting here writing.

The point I'm trying to make is that I am not genetically programmed to "not push, pull or lift anything more than ten pounds." That goes against my basic being.

Remember when a storm took out your electrical power and every time you went into another room you kept trying to turn on the lights? Well, that's me with the ten-pound thing. About every five minutes, I have an idea of something to do, only to have it smashed-to-hell by the ten-pound rule. Weigh some things around the house to see what your "less than ten-pounds" options are. Not many. But hey, I'm not totally helpless. There are some things I can do to help my wife who is bearing the brunt of all this. Let's see, I can carry out the plastic recyclables. Have to leave the bottles for Jennie. I can get the newspaper, except on Wednesdays when it is too heavy with department store sale inserts and coupons. Toilet paper needing changing? I'm all over it. I can help carry in the groceries as long as I get the last bag that has only bread. Can feed the dogs and cat as long as the forty-pound bag is already opened. Today I capped a gallon of strawberries.

On the negative side, my banjo weighs 14 pounds; my doghouse bass weighs 23 pounds; my hammered dulcimer weighs 18 pounds. Has anyone seen my harmonicas? Seeing my wife trying to start the weed-eater drives me crazy. I can't look. Have to go into the house.

I do have time to sit and think about problems that need solving. Yesterday I identified a problem, developed a solution, and solved it. Had to do with my catheter. Note: From the very beginning, I have been committed to telling the entire story regardless of how embarrassing or personal. So if I'm providing too much information for you, stop reading.

**The Catheter Problem** (women, children and the squeamish are advised to skip this section)

When a neighboring farmer bought a new Oliver 70 tractor, he would immediately start to weld, cut, and change it. He said that the idiot who designed the tractor obviously never plowed a day in his life. Well, the person who put in my catheter obviously never wore one a day in her life. The problem has to do with alignment. Gravity has decided that things should hang straight down. When things don't hang straight down, you are going against Mother Nature and the Tao, i.e., the natural order of things. Here's the problem. The part of the catheter that is attached to my leg is secured with medical duct-tape so it will not move. Great idea! But "where" it is secured and how far away from the other significant parts is crucial. In my case, the Tao was nowhere to be found. My little friend was hog-tied with no room to maneuver, always looking to the left---never in the position that nature intended. Well, I fixed that. A pair of scissors and my own duck tape put things in better alignment---my own catheter *Fung Shui*.

I am trying to approach these obstacles with as much acceptance and detachment as possible. My mantra is "It is as it is." So far I've done pretty well. The only thing that seems to get to me is not being physically and mentally detached from the catheter. I'm working on it. However, I admit that the catheter is providing me opportunities for growth, humility and humor. For example, yesterday the catheter provided a small existential experience. To accommodate the gallon-sized catheter bag, one must wear very loose underwear and pants. I threaded the bag and tubing through my underwear and down my left pant leg. Balancing myself on a door, I put the right leg in, put the right leg out, put the right leg in and shook it all about, etc. I put the left leg in, put the left leg out, etc., only to find that both legs ended up in the same hole. So there I was, standing alone in the bedroom with both legs in one pant leg. I took a deep breath and paused to let my emotions try to sort out what I should be feeling. I literally was caught somewhere between laughing and crying. *What's it all about, Alfie?*

# STRESS INCONTINENCE

*Whoops*

## Stress Incontinence: "The inability to control urination under <u>stressful</u> conditions."

A side effect of the surgery is temporary incontinence--- expect some level of incontinence for up to six months. Once my catheter was removed, I was eager to see where I stood in reference to "going with the flow."

I was pleasantly surprised when things seemed almost normal— normal when there was absolutely no stimulus occurring around me. I quickly learned that any sudden stimulus will trigger the "stress incontinence syndrome." And I mean any stimulus. Stress incontinence can best be explained by a joke.

A older man is telling his buddy about a recent bear-hunting trip.

"I was sitting on a log when I heard the brush rustling behind me. I remained perfectly still. The noise came closer and closer. I realized that something very large was just behind me. I slowly turned around and there stood an eight-foot bear with his front legs stretched into the air. It gave a horrifying growl."

To demonstrate the bear's behavior, the man stood up, stretched out his arms, made claws with his fingers, grimaced, and sounded a large *GRRRR*!!!" He paused and said, "I wet my pants."

"That's nothing to be ashamed of," said the friend, "Anyone would do the same when faced with a bear like that."

"No not then, just now, when I stood up and went--- *GRRRR*!!!"

With a full bladder, I would wet my pants just telling that joke. Speaking of jokes, karma just played one on me. As a teenager, I enjoyed making my mother laugh. I would tell a funny story, get her tickled, and watch her response. Because her female system had produced four children, she would clutch her apron between her legs and run to the bathroom while laughing uncontrollably. Like an elephant, karma remembers. My friend Gene and I have a similar sick sense of humor and always end up laughing when we get together. On his first visit after surgery, he was telling one of his crazy yarns when all three of us started laughing, Gene, my late mother and I.

I'm sure my mother was laughing as she peered over a heavenly cloud and watched me run to the bathroom holding myself. "Damn it Gene; either quit getting me tickled, or we'll need to swap shoes."

If your bladder is empty, all is well. But don't let a full bladder sneak up on you. With any significant bladder pressure, a sneeze, a cough, a laugh, or someone saying "Boo!" will cause the "stress reaction" to go into effect. There was a short learning curve concerning "trigger stimuli."

Free of the Foley Catheter, I was thrilled to go into the backyard, stand among the trees and relieve myself while overlooking the mountains. You men will understand—my wife doesn't. Here is the kicker. Planning to urinate is a stimulus. Have you noticed that the closer you get to a urinal the greater the urge? Well, as I prepared myself by unzipping my pants, taking a deep breath, looking at the scenery and savoring the moment, I glanced down and discovered that I had already been "going" without my knowledge or permission---straight down on my shoes. Obviously, the thought of going was enough stimulus to set things in motion without any awareness on my part. Lesson learned.

Along with stress incontinence comes the necessary "protection." As advertised on TV, I want to push my grandchild in a swing, walk on the beach and dance all night while feeling "secure"---reality is more challenging than as shown on TV.

From a Zen perspective, I am trying to be unashamed at what life offers me, regardless of societal traditions. Yet when it comes to incontinence, there is significant cultural baggage. For starters, the word "diapers"---and all its associations. But hey, astronauts wear them and they are not ashamed. My social worker friend tells me not to call them diapers but suggests I call them adult security pads, incontinence pads, or adult protective underwear. Obviously she has not talked with the Rite-Aid Drug Store recently because on aisle three, under the big blue sign that says "diapers" are my adult protective underwear.

Aisle three is complicated. The choices are confusing. How do I know which absorbency level, size, color or pad I need? Not one medical personnel has mentioned anything about this issue. I was on my own. I haven't felt that confused since the first time my wife sent me to the drugstore to purchase personal feminine products. I discovered there were twenty-three options---"The size of what?"

Shopping for protective underwear seems to bring up the theory of synchronicity, i.e., unrelated but meaningful events happening at the same time. Not sure I completely accept the theory, yet it does seem to rain right after I water my garden or wash my car. And the *Halleluiah Chorus* was on the radio at same time they took out my catheter. But here's the point. No matter what time of day, nor what drug store I select, important people in my life are always in line with me as I check out with my two boxes of "adult super-lined, feel secure, protective underwear." Believe me, protective underwear is not a conversation starter. At first it's all friendly, "How are you? Great to see you. How's retirement?"---until they spot what I am holding. I guess the "How are you?" is automatically answered by the box I'm holding. When they leave, they say something like, "Well, hang in there." Is that a Freudian slip? Obviously, they know.

A little philosophy: As I was sitting in the surgeon's waiting room with numerous other sick prostates, a gentleman next to me pointed to the diversity in race, ethnicity, and socio-economic statuses and said, "It's a great equalizer isn't it?" That statement really hit me. No matter how wealthy, powerful, religious or successful we are, life can quickly humble and equalize us. I think there is an immutable law of nature: *Feeling superior to others is impossible when you are wetting your pants.*

# COMPLICATIONS

*"Who knows Ms. Clockwork Orange's phone number?"*

The chances are Sally will not have a wreck while texting or smoker Sam will not get lung cancer or I will not have complications following surgery. Even though the consequences are dire, the statistical probabilities are in our favor.

Take those favorable odds and pile on the irrational belief that we are exempt from those grim predictions and you have a bunch of blind optimists running naked down the road of life. It's always the "others" who will suffer. It won't happen to me.

Is it optimism, hope, stupidity or maybe some genetic trick designed to weed out the gullible? Whatever it is, I have a bad case of it. I find it difficult, if not impossible, to believe negative probabilities will fall my way. And I was big-time wrong on this. My epitaph will read: "SELDOM IN DOUBT, OFTEN WRONG" or "I DIDN'T THINK I WAS THAT SICK."

I remember being told about the possibility of complications following surgery, the "bad" things that could happen---like the TV pharmaceutical warnings. I signed the consent form as if I were checking the box to abide by a Microsoft software agreement.

After the catheter removal ceremony, I was on the fast track to recovery until life decided to kick my over-confident ass.

**Complication # 1: Urinary Tract Infection**: The gift that keeps on giving.

A urinary tract infection comes with the catheter with no extra charges or shipping/handling fees. Only those men with a catheter are better able to relate to women who are accustomed to getting this condition. Usually it's only men with catheters who get the opportunity to empathize with their wives. My candid medical descriptions usually leave little to the imagination. However, in this case I will just say that the symptoms were "not desirable." So how will you know you have a urinary tract infection? You will know and so will your partner! To prevent a reoccurrence, I drank enough water to float the Delta Queen down Cripple Creek.

**Complication #2:** Bladder Neck Contracture or BNC for short.

Yes, that complication was on the list but the incident rate was only 3 percent---only three chances out of a hundred. I felt sorry for the three poor bastards who would experience it. Little did I know that the Sisters of Fate were pointing at me.

Without going into the gross medical details, a BNC is when your bladder, on its own accord and without your permission, decides not to allow any urine out—not now, not ever. Basically, the park is closed for the season.

So here is my "Tony needs humbling" experience. One Wednesday morning, I felt the call of nature and headed to my favorite spot in the backyard (We really live in the country). As I stood there trying to do what I normally do, I discovered that the fireman was ready but someone had obviously backed the truck over the hose or forgot to turn on the hydrant. Nothing, nada, zilch. Not a drop.

Now a female would have phoned a doctor right away. But not the male. When the car won't start, we spend forty-five minutes with the hood up, wiggling wires, looking intently at the motor hoping some flash of genius will come our way—while our wives call AAA. In the same vein, I thought that if I wiggled enough stuff, my pump would suddenly start running again.

"Let's see. I will drink a glass of water every thirty minutes. I need to exercise, to walk and work up a sweat. How about a beer? That always works. I'll take a hot shower. How about another beer?"

Nothing, nada, zilch. Not a drop. By this time it is early afternoon and I'm beginning to need maternity clothes but still refused to seek help. For males, going to the doctor is like having to read a map or ask directions. Remember the water balloons fights we used to have---when an overly inspired kid would fill a balloon with so much water that he couldn't get it out of the sink. Well, bingo—you've got the picture. Little did I know that I was not doing myself any favors by putting so much in when nothing was going out.

At some point even the male agrees to call AAA. At about 2:00 PM I had my "Oh crap, I'm in trouble" moment. I made an emergency call to the nearest urology office, jumped in the driver's seat and off we sped---with my wife's vocabulary limited to two words, "Slow down!" If having a baby is a five red-light buster, a kidney stone is a three; this was at least a two-lighter. To appease my wife, I ran only one red light. Where is Ms. Clockwork Orange when you need her? I was hurting.

When the receptionist asked to see my insurance card and handed me a clipboard with forms to fill out, I immediately knew that she did not fully appreciate the situation. So I let her, and a few nurses standing behind, know how we should be approaching the problem. Modesty and pain are inversely related. With enough pain, you don't care what you say, do, or who sees what. Anyway, the people in the lobby reading the two-year old Redbook magazines had something to talk about.

To get me out of the lobby as quickly as possible, a nurse took me back and began a test to determine the volume and capacity of my bladder. I told her she was wasting her time because it was "full—very full." When she read the numbers, she immediately called for another nurse to check it again. She did and immediately called for a doctor. At this point even the doc was fully engaged and things were picking up speed. We were all on the same page.

"Mr. Deal, we are sorry but we have to....."

"Go right ahead. Do whatever it takes!"

And they did. After several "un-sedated, un-successful" attempts to remedy the situation, the doctor sent a nurse to get a special apparatus. She came back with a coiled metal wire that looked familiar. "Where have I seen that before? Oh yes, the RotoRooter man." Glad he was in the building. The doctor's comment didn't make me feel any better. He held up the "apparatus" and said, "You'd better hope this works."

What transpired wasn't a pretty sight, but it worked and within fifteen minutes I had my color back, was sitting up, and was actually pleased to be holding hands with my old nemesis, Mr. Foley. I was one grateful and truly "relieved patient." Now there is new meaning to the old adage, "You don't miss your water until the well collapses" or something to that effect.

To understand what happened, I immediately scheduled an appointment with my surgeon, drove three hours only to learn, "Mr. Deal, we really don't know why it happened. It could be a combination of four or five things." If my understanding of combinations and permutations is correct, I have 126 possible things to worry about.    So for the next seven days, it's just me and Mr. Foley hobbling around the house driving my poor wife crazy.

Excuse me, someone's at the door.  "Well, it's Ms. Clockwork Orange.  Come in and have a seat."  All's well that ends well.

**Episode 16**

# SELF CATHETERIZATION

*You want me to do what?*

After my seven days, I sat in the third room on the left, pulling my 20 minutes until the doctor came. Designed waiting is built into medical practices. Uniformity is also a part of the system. Just as all McDonalds look the same in every state, so do urologists' offices. The lobbies, managed by the female office staff, are stocked with *Redbook, Southern Living, People Magazine* and some religious literature. A two-year waiting period is required before a particular edition is allowed in the lobby.

However, the reading material in the patient's room is obviously stocked by the doctors because there you find yachting and golfing magazines. Since I don't have a yacht or play golf, I am stuck spending my twenty minutes reading those god-awful, glossy, four-foot posters of a dissected man's internal organs—brought to you by Pfizer Drug Company. As if you are not depressed enough, you must sit and stare at an old man, cut in half with a finger stuck up his rear-end---illustrating a prostate digital exam. And the colors are those dreadful pinks, purples, and browns. A blown-up section of a dissected prostate, illustrating a microscopic view of cancer, is highlighted on the side. Wow, I really feel better spending twenty minutes staring at Mr. Poster-Boy.

After I served the required alone time, a nurse came in, gave me my paper robe, and laid out the instruments that will be involved with the *procedure du jour*—a procedure that most likely will involve our young nurse. Yet, this same nurse is concerned about my privacy while I am undressing and dressing.

"I'll leave you alone to change into the gown."

That statement came from one who is getting ready to hold my most private parts while the doctor does his thing. She doesn't want to see me pull up my underwear. "I'll pull this curtain while you dress." How nice!

Back to the medical stuff. The doctors finally think they understand my little bladder/urination problem. They have a fancy medical name for it, but I call it the "lower pierced ear syndrome." When you pierce an ear, the ear wants to grow the hole back shut. One has to keep something in the hole for it to remain open. The same is apparently true for the bladder neck opening. Since it has been wounded by surgery, it is growing scar tissue over the opening, the same opening that is vital to my being able to drink lots of beer. The doctors agreed that all we need to do is periodically put something into the opening to remind the body not to grow it shut. The pierced ear analogy holds true with the exception of the cosmetic results and the challenge presented by the hole location. However, their plan sounded reasonable enough.

"So let's do it. When is my next appointment?"

"Another appointment won't be necessary because we're going to show you how to catheterize yourself---daily for a week and then every couple of days thereafter for the next ten weeks."

Some words come packed with so much emotional information that the brain just can't muster enough synaptic firings for a complete understanding. I'm not talking about psychological denial because to deny, one must first understand. It's the tilt mechanism found in common pinball machines. The message is so profound that the brain is literally shaken off center, thereby producing that momentary blank stare, that pause, that deep breath, and that one four-letter word being held in reserve for such occasions.

*Mayday! Mayday! Mayday! We got problems in the left frontal lobe and we are sinking fast. Heavy stuff is flooding all rational compartments. Need more neurotransmitters sent up right away. And get more electrical stimuli up here ASAP!*

After the pause, my brain got it together enough to mumble, "Surely there's an alternative---some pills, exercise, or maybe another prayer shawl."

"A risky surgery is the only alternative."

Deep breath, long pause. "OK, show me how this will work."

Obviously the old "do it yourself" home repair trend has spread from Home Depot to the medical community. Not only did I have a drive-by operation, now I am going to be doing a "medical procedure" on myself. Aha! This is where the poster comes in. They will show me how to do this as illustrated on that stupid poster. No such luck. The lesson was going to be participatory. I was going to watch and learn. It was "show and *tail* time." Pun intended.

"Mr. Deal, I'm going to demonstrate what you'll do and then answer any questions you may have."

"That's great, Doc. Let me move so you can lie down on this table. I will stand where I can see you."

No such luck again. Believe me. I had a very close view. So the demonstration began—on me. The big concern in "the procedure" is to avoid infection through sterilization, cleanliness, and the correct handling of all involved "parts". Everything must be clean. Touch nothing unless it is sterilized. The doctor had several sterilized trays, rubber gloves, a white gown and a mask. The nurse also had sterilized attire and sterilized gloves, wipes, etc. They covered me with white sterilized paper with the exception of the circular, embarrassing, bulls-eye cutout. The "part" exposed by the cutout was cleaned with some orange sterile solution. Then they proceeded to demonstrate what I was supposed to do---on my own, by myself, in my "clean only when necessary" small bathroom. I noticed that the two of them together had four hands---all playing some critical role in what to touch and how to touch it. Last time I counted I had only two. May need to find two more hands. I had a long, lonely drive home. *"Noo...body knows the trouble I've seen; nobody knows my sorrow;"...."Nobody knows....."*

**For better or for worse, in sickness and in health for as long as you both shall live.** Yes, we said it, but the minister never mentioned this catheterization thing. In our thirty-seven years of marriage, Jennie and I have experienced about every "earthy" thing that could come with childbirth, breast-feeding, diapers, Montezuma's Revenge (diarrhea) gallbladder attacks, and overflowing toilets. I love her dearly and I trust her with my life. But ....... she is left-handed. I have seen her peel vegetables. And what part of the "procedure" would she do? Would we approach this like a well-oiled medical machine or argue like we are choosing which parking space to take. Is there a passive-aggressive tendency in her after all these years? Maybe this would bring us even closer as a couple? Or maybe she would never look at me, or a particular part of me, the same.

I know she would be at my side "for as long as we both shall live," and I know she would be a willing accomplice in this crime against my nature. But I can't ask her to do it. I'll drive my own get-away car. I'm on my own with this. After all, it's my thing—literally and figuratively.

# DO IT YOURSELF CATHETERIZATION

*"Bless his heart, he should've taken notes."*

**Note:** If you skipped Chapter 9, or don't know what self catheterization is, you may not fully understand the implications and gravity of a male having to do something so perverse to his best buddy—something that is prohibited by the Geneva Convention, i.e. indecent assault upon a person's body.

Self-Catheter Hymn #265

*"You gotta walk that lonesome valley; You gotta walk it by yourself; ……...Nobody else can do this for you, You gotta do it to yourself."*

It's just me in that lonesome valley---because I locked all the bathroom doors. Hope I can remember what they told me.

"Let's see, I'll need a baking pan for a tray, Tupperware bowl, paper towels, Dawn Antibacterial Hand Soap, rubber gloves, a handful of surgical jelly packets (packed by the same company that distributes the ketchup packets at Burger King), a washcloth, a sterilized catheter, tube of Lidocain ointment, a bottle of hydrogen peroxide, and **177 milliliters of George Dickel**. Think I'm ready."

And they said, "Methodically wash your hands before you begin." Check! Wait, I forgot to open the jelly packets---damn little things are so small and tough that I have to use my teeth. Oops, need to wash my hands again. Check!

And they said, "Use the special "insertion tip" on the tube of Lidocain ointment, and gently squeeze a small amount of jelly into 'yours truly' making sure the tip stays sterile." This is done for a minimum numbing effect---very minimum. Check. Oops. The Lidocain tube was on the back of the toilet and I touched it during the "gentle squeeze." Now I need to wash my hands again. Check!

"Damn it, Tony, you turned off the water with your hand. Now you've got to wash your hands again---use your elbows this time."

And they said, "Open the packet and remove the sterile catheter; making sure the catheter stays sterile." OK, I've got it but where can I put it that is sterile? Guess I'll hold one end of it between my teeth until I'm ready.

And they said, "Cover the catheter tube completely with the surgical jelly. While holding the catheter (with your sterilized hand), squirt the little surgical jelly ketchup packets onto the catheter." Sounds easy enough. Wrong. The jelly just sits there in little blobs and is not covering the catheter. And I'm not supposed to touch it. Maybe if I twisted it or shook it. "The tube must be completely covered all over or insertion will be painful!" I distinctly remember those words.

So there I sat, waiting until that thick honey slowly made its way down the tube, hoping for that "all-over" effect. Where is the Spray-On-PAM when you need it?

Oh crap! Because the jelly packets were on the side of the tub, my right hand (needed for the procedure) is now un-sterilized. Need to wash it again. Back to holding the catheter with my teeth. Hands are clean. Check. Now I'm ready.

And they said, "Use your left hand to hold the unwilling participant, use your right hand to insert the 14-inch catheter tube (pray it's completely covered with surgical jelly) until it enters the bladder."

Doc's warning: Sometimes it may be difficult to penetrate the bladder opening—especially if you are tense. If that happens, it might be helpful to hear running water. Yes, I was tense, and yes, it happened! So now I needed to turn on the faucet—how and with what? My two hands were definitely tied up at the moment. It's amazing what you can do with the toes on your right foot in an emergency. Glad the doors are locked. That had to look bad.

And they said, "Remember to stay relaxed." Oh, yes, I'm supposed to be very relaxed. Forgot that little bit of information. Relax General Custer, I'm sure the Indians just want to trade some beads.

Let's stop right here and explore what is wrong with this picture. One, the "completely covered" catheter is so slick that one can hardly hold it much less "control" it with any degree of accuracy. And accuracy is definitely called for. Secondly, it is physiologically and psychologically impossible to "stay relaxed" doing what I was doing. Thirdly, to do this procedure with only two hands is about as efficient as clapping with only one hand.

Well, my first wildcat drilling adventure did not strike oil. I gave up after thirty-eight minutes, nine hand washings, and numerous "oh shits." Glad my "friend" can't talk because I would've gotten an ear full. However, failure is not an option. Will drill again tomorrow. Need to re-think a few things. Should have taken better notes.

**Episode 18**

# SEEKING ADDITIONAL

# MEDICAL ADVICE

*It's all on YouTube.*

After the fiasco with my first self-catheterization, I left my naked male ego on the bathroom floor and decided to "stop and ask directions." Totally out of character for me. So, "Who you gonna call? Ghost Busters?" Wish I could. Ten years ago I would have called my doctor. But not in today's information age. Things are no longer that simple. Let me explain.

Since the day my local doc grimaced and said, "Hummm" as he checked my prostate, I have seen four different doctors in two different clinics, plus several interns and nurse practitioners. Being inquisitive, I asked each of them questions about my treatment, medications, prognosis, etc., only to find that "information" in this information age is obviously not getting around as fast as one would think. In other words, no one seems to tell me the same thing. Dr. A tells me to be sure to do X. Dr. B says, "For goodness sake, don't do X." Dr. C tells me to use lidocaine jelly to numb whatever I want to numb. Dr. D says that really doesn't work. I won't bore you with all the examples of differences in professional opinions—differences that could have significant consequences to me and yours truly.

Realizing the delicate nature of my relationship with doctors, I decided that I would be best served by not calling into question what each says. You don't want to get into pissing contests with urologists. Remember, urologists are experts in that area.

So what is a poor boy to do? Answer: Go on-line and ask Dr. Internet. The old e-Doc is just two clicks away. And that is exactly what I have been doing—with much success, I would add. It's amazing the number of people who use Dr. Google for their second and third opinions.

Do you realize how many catheterization videos there are on YouTube and how many chat-rooms are offering suggestions to catheter newcomers? "Hello. My name is Tony and I just completed my first self-catheterization." It's all there. No need to reinvent the wheel. Lots of good advice at a reasonable price…free. The world's largest library at your finger tips. However, one has to be selective about which book he pulls off the shelf. After watching 17 catheter videos and reading lots of advice recipes, I determined what I thought best and served up my own thing. So I am officially an "e-patient"---a patient who gets much of his medical information from YouTube and his Internet family.

A little advice about the Net. One, there are videos from all over the world. Even third world countries have the right to share their YouTubes. You might want to stay clear of any training video that uses live subjects, usually a brown, hairy-legged man (trying to earn some cigarette money) screaming as some female nurse (with no rubber gloves) does her thing to his thing. You don't need subtitles to know what is going on—moaning is the same in all languages. At the end of the video you get advice like:

- Don't share your catheter with others unless instructed by your health care practitioner.
- Don't do this as an experiment. Do this only if instructed by your medical provider.
- Make sure you have the right patient.
- If you can't remove the catheter, call for assistance.

And all very good advice! And I'm glad they told me. I was just getting ready to lend my catheter to my buddy, Gary, who was going to take it with him to the hunting lodge so the boys could "experiment" with it over the weekend. Advice from India sure put a stop to that. Sorry guys!

You know the video is a "Made in the USA" training video, if, instead of a live person, you see an anatomically correct mannequin. And I mean, really anatomically correct. Who makes those things anyway? And how do they advertise? Great conversation starter.

"And what do you do for a living?

"I design and manufacture penises. We make all types, sizes, colors, …"

"Excuse me, I think I hear my wife calling."

# Episode 19

# KEGEL EXERCISES

*You've been doing what behind my back?*

*"Mr. Deal, I'm recommending that you start doing kegel exercises daily."*

*"Great. Where's the gym?"*

I was handed a faded, single sheet outlining my prescribed exercise regimen—a regimen that was never taught in gym class. After the initial, "You squeeze what," I realized that the faded paper was not going to answer my questions. So back to Dr. Internet I go.

In the last chapter, I cautioned you about the importance of being selective in what you take from Dr. Net. Googling "kegel exercises" will quickly teach you the need for caution because you will get 1,030,000 hits telling you more than you ever wanted to know and offering options, testimonials, devices, videos, personal trainers and CDs. Remember the hairy-legged man from India!

To save you surfing time and embarrassment, I'll give you a brief summary of what I've learned.

- Kegel exercises (aka kegels), developed by Dr. Arnold Kegel, were designed to strengthen one's pubococcygeus muscle. That's right, the ol' pubococcygeus muscle. And I can't pronounce it either. That's why poor Doc Kegel got saddled with the term.

- Kegels were originally used to help women with urinary control after pregnancy. And like the first man who decided that eating a raw oyster would be a good idea, no one knows why the first man decided to try it. "Hey guys, I think I'll squeeze, hold, release, squeeze, hold, release, squeeze, hold, release" my pubococcygeus muscle for about six weeks and see what happens."

- And something did happen. Patients soon discovered an unintended consequence of buffing up the old pubococcygeus muscle---significant sexual benefits for both males and females---ergo, the million plus web sites selling Ronco Kegelcizers, vaginal barbells, etc.

- It is not clear how one knows that he/she is exercising the "right" muscle. Goodness knows the consequences if one inadvertently exercises the bulbocavernosus muscle instead! There are numerous Internet suggestions, videos, and apparati helping one find the correct muscle. Trust me, you do not want to explore or even visualize what is out there. Since we don't have a medical chart in front of us, I will enlighten you as to the proper muscle by examples. Visualize yourself in these male/female situations and be mindful of what muscle would be the first to move.

Male Example: Fred is hiking alone deep in the forest when he decides to stop and relieve himself. Just as he begins, a women steps out from behind a tree and says, " Fred, is that you?" Fred just kegeled!

Female Example: A nudist is walking down the beach. She is unaware of the large Doberman behind her as she bends over to pick up a seashell. Following an instinctive move on the dog's part, she kegeled. And, I might add, kegeled while setting the camp's long-jump record.

• There are two groups of people surfing for kegel information: old people looking for urinary control (that's me) and the young for sexual enhancement (that ain't me). According to the Net, if a kegeling young woman gets with a young man who kegels, the results could be....well, "Don't hang your pants on that cornstalk, we may not be coming down this row again."

• The beauty of kegels is that you can do them anywhere, anytime, and no one has to know. You don't have to waste your time at a social gathering, endure a boring sermon, or pretend to be listening to your spouse; you can be multi-tasking and kegeling at the same time. With facial muscle practice, you can actually look interested in the conversation when in reality you are counting kegel reps.

So now that I'm in the know when it comes to kegels, I realize that my wife has been kegeling behind my back. And I thought she was really listening to me.

# COMMUNICATION PROBLEMS

*I know you believe you understand what you think I said, but I'm not sure you realize that what you heard is not what I meant.*

I've put off the last several chapters hoping to have some up-beat news about the impact of prostate surgery on one's sex life. Obviously, I have not waited long enough. Yesterday, NPR's *Talk of the Nation* program had a noted author and a urologist discussing the disconnect between what patients optimistically heard about their post-surgery sexual functioning and what they ended up with six months later. Those who had prostate treatments were encouraged to call in and tell their story. The host was lucky that my cell phone battery was one of several things dead in my life.

Let's face it, prostate cancer is a money-making business. Before treatment, doctors are selling their goods and services without extended warranties. And yes, there are major communication breakdowns. In my case, I thought I heard, "We have an aggressive sexual rehabilitation program that will get you back in the saddle in no time." Since I was new at this, I had no idea what was involved in an "aggressive sexual rehabilitation program." I wasn't even sure about the "saddle" thing. Each time an attractive nurse would come in the room, my perverted mind wondered if she were involved in the program. "Excuse me, Miss. Would you happen to have your job description handy?"

I'm not totally blaming doctors for the miscommunication and the disconnect between what we expected and what we got. On the front end, they were selling and we were buying. Let's be honest.

Men are an easy sale when it comes to anything related to an optimistic view of sex. Being a student of psychology and having "duped" myself, I have given much thought about how this can happen. Save your research dollars. Here is my take on why there is a communication disconnect.

Reason Number 1. Men's brains are irrational---one oar is not fully in the water when it comes to sexual issues. Our perceptions and decisions are warped by our desires and expectations. The old saw is true: "The body does not have enough blood for both the brain and the penis to function at the same time." Pick your poison. We have visualized (daydreamed) ourselves being sexually competent for so long that we cannot comprehend the possibility that we may not (as the Viagra ad says) "Be ready when she is ready." The dismal odds, probabilities, and statistics just go right over our heads. We just feel sorry for the poor bastards who are affected by those statistics.

Reason Number 2. Men's brains are strongly influenced by habit and past experience. Surely it could not be too difficult to jump start a sluggish engine that has cranked up so easy for the last 57 years. Since that first discovery (courtesy of the Sears catalog and *National Geographic*), males have had daily erections—as sure as the sun comes up in the morning. For the most part, erections have occurred on command and sometimes without command, e.g., when accidentally touched by Mary Jo on the way to the blackboard in the sixth grade. A typical sixty-seven-year-old male has had approximately 26,805 erections in his lifetime, give or take a couple of special weekends. That is a lot of habit and brain memory to overcome. I wonder what Mary Jo looks like now?

Reason Number 3. The psychologist, Abraham Maslow, is famous for his theory of man's hierarchy of needs. Basically, his theory is that our needs are hierarchical. When we have met a lower set of needs, we move up the hierarchy to our next set of needs.... so on and so on until we are reading poetry and discussing the philosophy of Gandhi. Of course, our physical needs for air, water, food and shelter (staying alive) must be met before we move up the ladder to sex. However, a few of my friends have "hierarchy-ed" sex somewhere between air and water. Unfortunately, that is also their standard for a willing partner...that she is breathing.

Anyway, back to Abraham. When you think you are dying of prostate cancer, your brain puts sex on the back burner. Reading those life expectancy tables sure deflates a man, literally and figuratively. But no sooner than the doctor says, "I think we got it all," you start looking around for that good-looking nurse. Then, and only then, are you concerned how the "captain" came through the operation. For most males, fear of dying supersedes sex, but not by much and not for long. Note: Exception to this rule is one of my friends, who, I'm sure, will be hitting on his hospice nurse.

Reason Number 4. Proverbs said it best: "Pride cometh before a fall." Maybe it is an evolutionary by-product, but the reality is that men are prideful of and lie about their sexual prowess. The competition starts at Boy Scout camp and continues until the final dirt-nap. We begin to believe our own story about quantity, quality, and size of our Harley-Davidsons. So when the doc lays out the gloomy sexual odds, each of us believes that we are better than the rest...that our engine has more horsepower...that we get more miles to the gallon and that the women are impressed with our five-speed gear shifter. "Sure it's been a long six months, but I'm positive it will fire right up."

# Episode 21

---

# SEX IN THE CITY

*But I live in the country.*

The hospital's "aggressive sexual rehabilitation program" was dangled before me like some carrot (probably a poor choice of words). But the idea was intriguing and was one more rung that made it easier to climb into the surgery wagon—a wagon that knowingly would have a bumpy sexual ride.

**A little anatomy lesson**: The bad-guy, cancerous prostate, is surrounded by a posse of numerous hair-like nerves. It's impossible to capture the prostate without collateral damage to these nerves— leaving one's erector-set a few pieces shy. For most patients, these damaged nerves get their act back together in about six months. Of course, this depends on the extent of the cancer, its location, and whether the surgeon had too many cups of coffee that morning.

Even the best scenario will send a patient on a six-month sexual sabbatical, a little hiatus from the heavy work of daily erections. For some wives, this is also seen as a sabbatical—one that results in a reduction of Saturday night headaches.

However, this six-month hiatus is not without some serious physical consequences—ergo, the need for an aggressive sexual rehabilitation program. The main problem has to do with atrophy--- the old "use it or lose it" syndrome. It seems the male sex organ can't go without exercise for six months and then expect to be on top of its game. When *reveille* is blown, there must be a morning flag-raising ceremony or the soldier will think the war is over and go home. So the Sexual Rehab Program is do or die---especially if the soldier has been on duty for 67 years. To keep things in shape, the rehab program offers drugs, machines (that's right, machines), education, exercises, and counseling (to adjust to new sexual roles).

Now that I have your attention, I'll describe some aspects of the program and share a few things that happened to a "friend" who is in the program.

The first line of defense was from the pharmacy---two different types of pills. I'm sure you've seen all the Viagra-type advertisements on TV. My "friend" got the first prescription, swallowed a pill and then looked for two old timey claw-foot tubs in which he and his wife could sit naked and watch the sunset. Not having two tubs, they resorted to squeezing themselves into their one small tub and lighting a few candles. The evening did not go as advertised. My "friend" said they were just grateful that they could get back out of that slippery tub without hurting themselves.

The second pill was a next generation pill that costs twenty-four dollars each (insurance doesn't pay). Now I admit I'm a little tight when it comes to money. Like the granite counter tops, I began to question just how badly I wanted this " therapy" and thought about how many banjo strings I could buy with the cost of one pill. This is where the second program component comes into play, the machine. The Doc knows that most men will not pay twenty-four dollars a day to exercise his buddy, so a machine (paid for by your tax dollars—

thanks!) was prescribed---that's right, a patented, Ronco, three battery, portable, vacuum therapy system with size adapters, an easy loading system, a leather carrying case, instructional DVD, and other unique features (my model doesn't come with lights or a place to plug in your Ipod). I thought the doc was joking when he described this bionic connection. But he was serious. It's definitely a "don't try this at home---for professionals only" type of exercise. The manual strongly recommended that the new owner try this machine alone for few weeks before involving his partner. Good advice, damned good advice!

Like most men, I usually skip written instructions. But this is one time I watched that DVD several times and read the manual until the pages were worn. Took no chances! This therapy is not for the squeamish. Having lived through the sixties and seventies, I thought I had seen and done it all. Well, add one more to my "you ain't gonna believe what I just did" list. Now all I have to do is to develop a "check-out" system to keep up with which one of my friends borrowed the machine last. Let's see, I think it was last in Granite Falls.

Another component of the therapy was an educational examination about the birds and the bees. With my age and experience, I knew I would ace it. Wrong!

**Question:  What is the largest sex organ?**  I <u>proudly</u> penciled in my "incorrect" answer.  Correct answer:  The skin.

**Question:  What is the most important sex organ?**  Again I was wrong.  Correct answer:  The brain.

**Question:  What increases the more a man has sex?**  Disappointed and wrong again.  Answer:  His life expectancy.

**Question:  What is the relationship between headaches and sex?**  Wrong again.  Answer:  Sex releases endorphins and relieves headaches.

**Open-ended question:** *Describe an effective foreplay technique for your wife.*  Wrong again (but I enjoyed giving my answer).  Correct answer: Go with her to ***Bed, Bath and Beyond*** and help her pick out pillow-shams for the guest bedroom, then take her out to a candle-light dinner and really listen to what she says.  (Would have never guessed that one!)

After the little quiz, the doc shared why it is important to continue having "intimate physical contact" during this six-month period. Even though the male may be "back in the saddle" after six months, his wife may have become too accustomed, and too comfortable, with the break. The old None Nun Syndrome. So the doc says it is important to keep the fires burning, to do something during this period, even if it is radically different from the usual.

So guess what! For the next six months or so, my wife and I are "going steady." I'm sure no one under the age of fifty will understand the significance of that official designation. But for our generation, going steady was a big deal. We are back to doing all the "going steady" things we used to do behind the high school bleachers and in the back seat of our parents' car---lots of going to second and third base without ever doing "it." And guess what, it's great. I might even ask her to the prom.

Remember those "Quality of Life Questionnaires?" Now I have some information to provide. Think I'll call them back.

**Episode 22**

# AND THEY LIVED HAPPILY
# EVER AFTER

*Having a frog that talks*

*"How's your wife?"*

*"Compared to what?"*

"Tony, how are you doing?"

"Doing great," is my usual reply. And in the scheme of things, that answer is pretty accurate. But great is relative—**compared to what?**—soon after surgery or when I was sixteen?

Even though I am doing great, I need to change the old saw, "I'm not as good as I once was, but I'm as good once as I ever was" **to** "I'm not as good as I once was, but with my Ronco, portable, twin battery, vacuum therapy system with size adapters, easy loading system, a leather carrying case, and instructional DVD, I'm good as long as my batteries last."

Yes, the bar has been lowered. Father Time has a way of lowering the bar for all of us. Having prostate cancer just nudges that process along a little faster. But to be perfectly honest, my priorities have shifted. I'm not the same. I am more content today to sit in those twin claw-foot tubs, hold my wife's hand, look at the sunset, have a glass of wine, and talk about our grandchildren. The old frog joke pretty much sums it up.

An elderly man, strolling through the woods, sat down on a log to rest. A frog hopped up on the log and said, "Hey mister, kiss me, and I will turn into a beautiful woman who will be at your beck and call." With a startled look, the old man reached down, grabbed the frog, put it in his pocket and continued walking. The frog cried out, "Didn't you hear me?" The old man stopped, pulled open his pocket with his fingers, looked at the frog and said, "I heard you---but at my age, I would rather have a talking frog."

It's not *if* but **when** all of us would rather have a frog that talks. Life will change us, either slowly or abruptly. We all are just one phone call, one medical test away from a changed life. My life's trajectory was changed without my permission. But to fight this change would not only be futile, but also would diminish the wonderful rollercoaster ride our Creator has made for us. It is as it is!

Sometimes when humbled by life, I remember a profound statement uttered by a young student of mine. She was on a college backpacking trip into the Linville Gorge Wilderness Area with my class when we got "sort-of" lost. "Sort-of" getting lost in the gorge is like being half-pregnant. Anyway, after several days of walking in high heat and humidity, bushwhacking through rhododendron thickets, and running low on water, she started jettisoning her valuable possessions in order to lighten her backpack---"things" no longer meant anything to her. After lots of scratches, tears and four-letter words, this city girl finally found civilization. Later, when she was describing her horrible experience, her mother asked, "Why didn't you just quit?" The girl looked at her mother and said, "I would have, <u>but **there was no place to quit to!"**</u>

How true of life. Sometimes life sets us on a journey in which there is "no place to quit to." Cancer is one such journey. Even though we may have no choice about which trip we are given, we can choose how we will approach it. We can be creative and upbeat. That's what I have tried to do for the last six months as I stood naked before you (figuratively speaking) and laughed at myself. I literally exposed myself---describing my experiences with finger exams, catheters, machines, leakage, pain, urinary tract infections, drugs, etc. I have tried to stay out of the self-pity box and to see illness in a different way.

One of my favorite examples of seeing differently comes from a four-year-old boy. During a T-ball game, he closely watched the batters before him. When it came his turn at bat, he stepped up to the plate, took a big swing, hit the ball and ran as fast as he could.... straight to third base. His embarrassed parents hid their faces. Later when asked why he ran to third base, he said, "Well, when you run to first base, they get you out." He was a problem solver, an outside the box thinker and saw that some behaviors just didn't work. Following his insight and bravery, we should all change our approach to our health issues---and try running to third base instead of first.

Our choice is either being angry at life, feeling cheated, and rejecting what is or having a positive attitude, a sense of humor, and accepting what is. The power of positive thinking, hope, and laughter can change the destination of our journey. Remember, it's impossible to laugh and die at the same time.

During these six months, I have been a student. While I've learned much about illness and prostate cancer, I have learned more about healing—about the power of touch from a doctor or nurse, the power of a smile, the power of laughter, the power of love from friends and family and, just maybe, the power of Mt. Zion's Prayer Tree.

*"A mind that is stretched by a new experience can never go back to its old dimensions."* Oliver Wendell Holmes

# ABOUT THE AUTHOR

Tony Deal, PhD, is a retired educator who lives with his wife in Western North Carolina. Other than managing the "to do list," he spends his time playing old-time and bluegrass music, building greenways, laughing with his granddaughters, and volunteering for Hospice. In 2004, he received the National Hospice Volunteer of the Year Award.

Tony can be reached at: tonyraydeal@gmail.com

Made in the USA
Middletown, DE
10 January 2015